IS IT ...

TO YOU?

IS IT NOTHING TO YOU?

The Unchanging Significance of the Cross

Frederick S. Leahy

THE BANNER OF TRUTH TRUST

THE BANNER OF TRUTH TRUST
3 Murrayfield Road, Edinburgh EH12 6EL, UK
P.O. Box 621, Carlisle, PA 17013, USA

*

© Frederick S. Leahy 2004

ISBN 0 85151 877 X

*

Typeset in 10$^{1}/_{2}$/14 pt Sabon at the
Banner of Truth Trust, Edinburgh
Printed in Great Britain by
Bell & Bain Ltd.,
Glasgow.

Contents

Foreword

Commenting on Paul's words in 1 Corinthians 1:7, John Calvin wrote, 'All the wisdom of believers is comprehended in the cross of Christ.' I cannot but think that Frederick Leahy would assent to these words for two reasons: his admiration for the theology and exegetical insights of the Reformer, and his own experiential proclamation over several decades of the importance of the cross of Jesus Christ. Those readers familiar with Fred Leahy's other titles (*The Cross He Bore, The Victory of the Lamb* and *Satan Cast Out*) will already know of this author's esteem for the cross of Christ. In this new volume we find, in addition, the passion of an evangelist.

Professor Leahy (for this is how I have always known him) is a 'Prince in Israel'. More than one generation of preachers have sat at his feet at the Reformed Presbyterian Church's theological college in Belfast and profited from his wisdom combined with a gentlemanly humility that suffused his teaching and preaching with the fragrance of Christ.

Though I was never one of his students, I owe more to Fred Leahy than he probably knows: a letter he wrote to me almost a decade ago influenced my own pathway to the 'academy'. In it he gently but firmly urged me to pursue my own interest in a particular field of study whilst at the same time supplying a list of possible sources that 'might prove to be helpful'. They were!

I have known him for a quarter century, and known of him for almost as much again. He is a theologian and preacher – No! A preacher-theologian. If the best theologians are first of all preachers, then Fred Leahy must be among the finest of theologians. Readers of this volume will uncover his patient exegesis, his theological sensitivity and his evangelist's heart. The very title breathes the passion of an evangelist! The chapters that follow are a meditation on the successive stages of the sufferings of Christ in his final hours in Gethsemane and Calvary. As such, they bear the hallmarks of considerable meditation on what is central and most significant in the passion of Christ.

There is a wisdom that comes with great age. The 81-year-old pianist, Tatiana Nikolayeva, in a recent recording of Shostakovich's *Twenty-Four Preludes and Fugues, Opus 87*, is said to breathe something of an 'authority that is majestic', finding 'depths . . . which have eluded most other pianists'. Commenting on Peter's confession at Caesarea Philippi in Matthew 16, Calvin added, 'The minds of men are destitute of that sagacity which is necessary for perceiving the mysteries of heavenly wisdom which are hidden in Christ . . . till God opens our eyes to perceive his glory in Christ.' As the glory of Christ shines in these pages one is grateful that God has opened the eyes of this octogenarian author to impart wisdom to the rest of us. He tells me it is his 'last' book. But, as preachers may be forgiven the repetition of 'finally' in a sermon, so forgiveness will be forthcoming if this proves not to be his last word.

DEREK W. H. THOMAS
John E. Richards Professor of Systematic and Practical Theology,
Reformed Theological Seminary, Jackson, Mississippi.

Introduction

This book is dedicated to my colleagues in the Reformed Theological College, Belfast. With one exception, the chapters were originally sermons, now somewhat enlarged. This is no mere academic exercise: I have two deep concerns. The first is that Christians need to realize the value of meditation on the Word of God. Reading the Bible and being familiar with its contents is necessary, but for spiritual growth and maturity, not enough.

There is no place for speculation in the definition of Christian doctrine – we are limited by what has been revealed – but in meditating on God's Word and in preaching it, there is a place for our God-given imagination within the bounds of the biblical record. Pierre Marcel comments helpfully: 'When in preaching, a man abandons himself to the freedom of the Spirit, he discovers that his faculties are developed above normal: freedom is given not only to the soul but also to the tongue, his mental penetration is deeper; his ability to picture things in his mind is greater; truth works a greater power in his soul; his faith is more intense; he feels himself involved in a living and compact reality.'[1] What is true of preaching is equally true of meditation, provided such freedom is governed by the facts recorded in God's Word.

[1] Quoted by Joseph A. Pipa Jr, 'Puritan Preaching', in *The Practical Calvinist* (Fearn: Christian Focus Publications, 2002), p. 177.

My second concern is for the unconverted, including the seeker after truth. Can the death of a great Teacher some two thousand years ago have any relevance for our present distraught world and for our personal lives? Many can see no relevance whatsoever. The aim of this book is to show that Christ's death and resurrection have a powerful and timeless message for humankind. The cross of Christ stands in Scripture as the pivot on which all history turns, the fulcrum from which the battlements of Satan are toppled. A day is coming when that will be made plain to all. As Paul said to the wise men of Athens, '[God] has fixed a day on which he will judge the world in righteousness by a man whom he has appointed, and of this he has given assurance to all by raising him from the dead' (*Acts* 17:31).

I am much indebted to the insights of the Dutch theologian, Klaas Schilder, whose seminal ideas can be amplified and applied.

Except when otherwise stated, the translation of Scripture employed is the English Standard Version.

I wish to thank Edward Donnelly, Principal of the Reformed Theological College, Belfast, for reading the manuscript and for helpful suggestions, which I was happy to adopt. Also I am grateful to Professor Derek Thomas of the Reformed Theological Seminary, Jackson, Mississippi, for his Foreword, to the editorial team of the Banner of Truth Trust for their help, to my sister-in-law, Eileen, who deciphered and typed my handwriting, and to my wife, Margaret, who encouraged me to write this book and for her interest in the work.

FREDERICK S. LEAHY
May 2004

1

What Is the
Shepherd Worth?

Palestinian shepherds had no social standing, many being no more than mere hirelings, but a good shepherd, like David, displayed commendable qualities. He cared for and protected his sheep. If one of a hundred were missing, he would search diligently for it, not resting until he had found it. He would give his life for his sheep (*John* 10:11). In the Old Testament God is likened to a shepherd, and our Lord said, 'I am the good shepherd.'

Through the ages God has raised up godly men to serve his church as under-shepherds, teaching his people by word and example. God's spiritual shepherds, the prophets, were seldom valued. In Zechariah 11:12 we are startled to read that the prophet of God was valued at only thirty pieces of silver. Thirty pieces of silver! An insulting valuation – the price of a slave gored by an ox (*Exod.* 21:32). This phrase resonates in the New

Testament. The rejection of God's true prophets foreshadowed the rejection of Christ; their evaluation was repeated in the paltry sum paid to Judas. To see this in perspective, we need to step back in history.

To be deported *en masse* from one's homeland by a great world power, and taken a thousand miles to a foreign land with a different culture and religion, and to remain there for a whole generation, would be a horrendous experience. That is what happened to the Jews when taken captive by Nebuchadnezzar, King of Babylon, in 605 BC. The poet Byron described the heartbreak of these people.

> *We sat down and wept by the waters*
> *Of Babel, and thought of the day*
> *When our foe, in the hue of his slaughters,*
> *Made Salem's high places his prey;*
> *And ye, oh her desolate daughters!*
> *Were scatter'd all weeping away.*

The exile had been foretold by Micah (*Mic.* 4:10) and Isaiah (*Isa.* 39:6). Jeremiah prophesied that the captivity would last seventy years (*Jer.* 25:11–12); and it did. In 538 BC, Cyrus, king of Persia, who had conquered Babylonia, issued a decree authorizing the Jews to return to the land of their fathers and to rebuild the Temple (*Ezra* 1:1–4). Over 42,000 of them embraced the opportunity (*Ezra* 2:64). Imagine the joy and expectation of those people and their shock when they saw their beloved Jerusalem in ruins.

At first there was much zeal and enthusiasm as they undertook the task of rebuilding the walls of the city. Yet all was not well. That early fervour began to wane. The walls of Jerusalem were rebuilt; but the Temple remained virtually in ruins while the people were busy building luxurious dwellings for themselves. Material walls had been rebuilt; but there were spiritual walls that had been neglected.

At this critical time, the prophet Haggai appeared on the scene rebuking the people for their materialism. God's word conveyed by his prophet struck home. 'Is it a time for you yourselves to dwell in your panelled houses, while this house [the Temple] lies in ruins?' (*Hag*. 1:4). The people did respond and resumed the work of restoring God's house.

In his ministry, Haggai was ably supported by the prophet Zechariah, who called the people to repentance and spoke of the grace of God and his purposes of redemption. The name Zechariah means 'Jehovah remembers'. The main thrust of his prophecy is summed up in the words, 'Return to me, says the LORD of hosts, and I will return to you . . .' (*Zech*. 1:3). There were in Israel at that time those who might be termed 'Israelites indeed', as well as those who had returned to Palestine motivated by a sense of worldly pride and advantage. Those who were sincere in heart needed encouragement: the insincere needed rebuke and an earnest call to repentance. Zechariah's ministry met these needs. He was fearless in declaring that God's indignation had been

[3]

aroused by the people's sin, while holding out assurance of blessing if they repented. But above all, he pointed to the blessing that would come through the promised Messiah. Zechariah was a faithful under-shepherd caring passionately for the people of God; but such a witness is not without its cost.

GOD'S PROPHET EVALUATED

There were two kinds of prophets in Israel – the false and the true; the hirelings and the faithful shepherds; those sent by God and those self-appointed shepherds who proclaimed the dreams of their own hearts. Jeremiah had warned against the pernicious influence of such men. 'Thus says the LORD of hosts, "Do not listen to the words of the prophets who prophesy to you, filling you with vain hopes. They speak visions of their own minds, not from the mouth of the LORD. They say continually to those who despise the word of the LORD, It shall be well with you; and to everyone who stubbornly follows his own heart, they say, No disaster shall come upon you"' (*Jer.* 23:16–17).

Such self-seeking men hindered the work of the true prophets. That was the situation in Zechariah's day. Most of the people preferred the charm and the soft words of the false prophets to the seemingly austere message of God's servant. Zechariah was well aware of the havoc wrought by the false prophets. Israel had been unfaithful to her covenant obligation. So, in what were probably a vision and a prediction that would find its ultimate fulfilment in Christ, Zechariah announced a formal severing of relations with them, symbolized by the breaking of his staff (*Zech.* 11:10).

Zechariah had been rejected. His message had been despised. So there came that moment when he said, 'I will not be your shepherd' (*Zech.*11:9). Then came the challenge, 'If it seems good to you, give me my wages; but if not, keep them' (*Zech.*11:12). He was virtually saying, 'Pay me what you think I am worth, or else keep it. Evaluate me. What has my ministry among you been worth? Of what value has my message been? Do you wish me to minister further among you, or do you prefer to follow the hirelings? Make up your minds. Tell me where I stand, and where you stand'. 'Give me my wages'. 'And they weighed out as my wages thirty pieces of silver' (*Zech.* 11:12).

That payment was an ignominious insult and an outright rejection of God's prophet. It was an expression of disdain. By it the people showed how utterly unworthy they were of one whose faithful witness they had scorned. Thirty pieces of silver was the compensation paid for an injured slave (*Exod.* 21:32)! They treated God's prophet and shepherds as they would a common slave. That was how they esteemed the Word of God conveyed by his servant. That was their evaluation of his prophet. But in mocking the prophet, they were mocking God. So God, in turn mocks them as he intervenes and instructs Zechariah to take the money and 'throw it to the potter', Zechariah adding ironically, 'the lordly price at which I was priced by them' (*Zech*. 11:13). 'Throw it to the potter'! This may well have been a proverbial expression for the disposal of something of no value or use; but it is much more likely that Zechariah had a passage from Jeremiah in mind. 'Arise, and go down to the potter's house, and there I will let you hear my words' (*Jer*. 18:2). From Jeremiah 19:2 we learn that Jeremiah was sent 'to the Valley of the Son of Hinnom at the entry of the Potsherd Gate', in order to proclaim God's word in that place. That valley lay adjacent to the Temple. Jeremiah had to convey a chilling message from God. 'Behold, I am bringing such disaster upon this place that the ears of everyone who hears it will tingle . . . So will I break this people and this city, as one breaks a potter's vessel, so that it can never be mended' (*Jer*.19:3,11). To Zechariah, those pieces of silver, like the broken vessels of Jeremiah's potter, were a symbol of the people's guilt and impending judgement. Zechariah is represented as obeying the Lord's command, doing so publicly in 'the house of the LORD', for this transaction involved the people's standing before God. When we turn to the New Testament, we see that this passage is Messianic in character and in his actions, Zechariah is a type of Christ.

GOD'S SON EVALUATED

Clearly Zechariah's vision was prophetic of the manner in which Christ, the divine Prophet, was regarded. The Holy Spirit has built a bridge between Zechariah's vision and Matthew's account of the betrayal of Christ. All four

Gospels record Judas' treachery, and Matthew, Mark and Luke speak of Judas as 'one of the Twelve', emphasizing the evil nature of his act. It was one of Christ's closest followers who betrayed him. 'He who ate my bread has lifted his heel against me' (*John* 13:18). Both Luke and John link Satan with the act of Judas as he went to the high priest and his associates asking, 'what will you give me if I deliver him over to you?' They paid him thirty pieces of silver! (*Matt.* 26:15).

The harsh prophecy of five hundred years earlier had been fulfilled. How astounding that these religious leaders in Jerusalem, learned in the Scriptures, should now unwittingly prove the truth and validity of Zechariah's prophecy by being the instruments in its fulfilment. Other good men had been betrayed before, and good men have been betrayed since; but this treachery was unique, for Christ admits of no comparison. He stands at the centre of history: the Son of God and the Son of man, the foundation and crown of the Church.

This was shameful commerce as the blood of Christ was sold for thirty pieces of silver. That was how the leaders of Israel evaluated Christ. As we try to visualize the scene – the sly Judas and the astute priests – we are filled with disgust. Even to the natural eye, the scene is repulsive. Yet with spiritual vision we detect the presence of another Person and hear him say, 'Give me my price – what am I worth to you? How do you evaluate me?' It is the voice of Christ. And look! They carefully count out thirty pieces of silver. God let those silver coins drop down through the centuries, and now the priests hand them, so to speak, to Judas. Look carefully at what happened to those accursed coins - 'the reward of iniquity' as Peter called them (*Acts* 1:18, KJV). In a moment of dark and hopeless remorse, this 'son of perdition' (*John* 17:12, KJV) brought the money back to the chief priests saying, 'I have sinned by betraying innocent blood' (*Matt.* 27:4). But he was met with scorn and derision as the priests replied coldly, 'What is that to us? See to it yourself'. The fact that these priests had paid money for innocent blood did not bother them. As far as they were concerned, Judas' conscience was his problem. He had been their tool and now they discard him, and Satan discards him too! So Judas hurls the money at them in the Temple, rushes out and commits suicide. His evil transaction had proved to be double-edged:

> Still, as of old,
> Man by himself is priced.
> For thirty pieces Judas sold
> Himself, not Christ.

Then these religious men, so good at swallowing camels and straining out gnats (*Matt.* 23:24), took the money which could not be returned to the treasury, because it was 'blood money', and purchased 'the potter's field' for the burial of foreigners - long known as 'the Field of Blood'.[1]

---

[1] The difference between remorse and repentance is noteworthy. In remorse, the sinner is sorry for himself; in repentance the sinner

In recording this procedure, Matthew gives a free quotation from Zechariah 11:13. 'Then was fulfilled what had been spoken by the prophet Jeremiah, saying, And they took the thirty pieces of silver, the price of him on whom a price had been set by some of the sons of Israel, and they gave them for the potter's field, as the Lord directed me' (*Matt.* 27:9–10). There are two possible explanations for Matthew attributing this passage to Jeremiah. It was common practice for the Jews to name an Old Testament writing after the first book in a scroll. Zechariah happened to be in the scroll whose first book was Jeremiah. But when we recall that Zechariah seems to have passages like Jeremiah 18 and 19 in mind when recording the words 'Throw it to the potter' and in his subsequent action, it is probable that 'the Evangelist had in his eye the inseparable connection between the prediction in Zechariah and the earlier announcements in Jeremiah . . .'[2] Whichever explanation is taken, it is clear that there is no contradiction here, or lapse of memory. The vital fact remains that what Zechariah's vision typified came to pass. Jesus of Nazareth, God's Son, was valued at a derisory price.

---

is sorry for his sin. Overcome by remorse, Judas took his own life. Seeing his sin for what is was, an affront to the holy nature of God, Peter, in true repentance, 'went out and wept bitterly'.

[2] Patrick Fairbairn, *Hermeneutical Manual* (Edinburgh, T. & T. Clark, 1858), p. 444.

It is not just worldly churchmen and intellectuals who devalue the Son of God; this world has no room in its thinking for One who is seen as irrelevant to its needs. When the United Nations HQ was being built in New York, there was some controversy as to whether a place of worship should be included in the building. An American newspaper carried a cartoon depicting a huge Hand (God). In the centre of the Hand was a small globe (the world), on top of the globe stood a group of little men having a heated argument. The caption read, 'Do we have to invite Him, as well?' The second Psalm represents God as laughing at the arrogance of puny, sinful man.

GOD'S GRACE EVALUATED

Zechariah's message, like that of all God's prophets, was one of sovereign grace. He proclaimed salvation by the grace of God and pointed to the redemptive work of his Son. The prophets as a whole spoke of a suffering Saviour and of his redeeming blood. Human merit had no place in the obtaining of forgiveness: all was of grace. So Zechariah did not say, 'You must turn over a new leaf and try to live in a more upright way. Get back to basics.' No. Instead he said 'Repent.' 'Do not be like your fathers to whom the former prophets cried out, "Thus says the LORD of hosts, Return from your evil ways and from your evil deeds." But they did not hear or pay attention to me, declares the LORD. Your fathers, where are they? . . .' (*Zech.* 1:4-5). The call to repentance is one of grace; but sinful man, in and of himself, turns a deaf ear to that loving call. He does not 'hear or pay attention'. He places no value on the grace of God.

In Zechariah's time, the people decided that they did not need the ministry of God's shepherd. They felt they could manage quite well on their own. Self-redemption was at the heart of their creed. They chose to be guided by their own light. The element of grace had been abandoned. They no longer wanted an Owner. They would be their own lords and masters. 'Pay off Zechariah! Give him the price of a slave. We do not need him or his teaching'. Well does Klaas Schilder comment, 'The thirty pieces are the tangible embodiment of the spirit of self-redemption. Grace allows no glorying in the self. Redemption is from Thee, from Thee alone.'[3]

During Christ's ministry were the reactions of his hearers different from those who heard Zechariah? Was his word of grace valued highly? Did men recognize his infinite worth and the wonder of saving grace? Did they turn away from the idea of self-redemption? Not at all. They trusted in their own righteousness and spurned the loving call of grace; for grace leaves no room for glorying in self, and sees redemption coming from God in matchless mercy and love - wholly undeserved. In Scripture, man's imagined righteousness is seen as 'a polluted garment' (*Isa.* 64:6) – just rags and tatters in the sight of a holy God.

---

[3] Klaas Schilder, *Christ in His Suffering* (Grand Rapids, Wm. B. Eerdmans, 1945), p. 79.

We are left with the crucial question, 'What think ye of Christ?'

Well did John Newton write:

> *What think ye of Christ is the test,*
>   *To try both your state and your scheme;*
> *You cannot be right in the rest*
>   *Unless you think rightly of him.*
>
> *As Jesus appears in your view,*
>   *As he is belovéd or not,*
> *So God is disposéd to you*
>   *And mercy or wrath are your lot.*

As we reflect on this theme, those thirty pieces of silver are before us. God rattles them in our ears – the world's estimate of Christ! And Christ is saying to us, 'Give me my price. What am I worth to you? Is my blood precious to you? Is my grace treasured by you?' Our answer indicates our eternal destiny.

2

A Crucial Vote

During the American Civil War, the poet James Russell Lowell, wrote the well-known lines:

Once to every man and nation comes the moment
to decide.
In the strife of Truth with Falsehood, for the good
or evil side . . .

One outstanding moment of decision, with far-reaching consequences for Jew and Gentile alike, was when Pilate faced a frenzied crowd and asked, 'Whom do you want me to release for you: Barabbas, or Jesus who is called Christ?' (*Matt.* 27:17). Pilate was trying desperately to free this Prophet from Nazareth. He was convinced of his innocence (*Luke* 23:4). There was some indefinable quality about this Man that made the astute Roman Governor uneasy, even afraid. His superstitious pagan nature had been aroused by an urgent message from his wife: 'Have nothing to do with that righteous man, for I have suffered much because of him today in a dream' (*Matt.* 27:19). Pilate was an experienced administrator. To him politics was the art of the possible. He was pragmatic, hard-headed, governed by expediency rather than principle. He thought he knew these agitators, whom he regarded as hot-blooded, fanatically religious Semitic peoples ready to flare up over some petty annoyance. This was not the first time they had caused him trouble. Now he is losing control. The priests and people press him hard. He resorts to one ploy after another, but all in vain.

THE PERVERSE DECISION

Pilate remembered the established custom at the Passover season to release, as an act of grace, any one prisoner chosen by the people (*Matt.* 27:15). At that time there was a notorious prisoner called Barabbas. Mark tells us that this man was a rebel and a murderer (*Mark* 15:7) and John calls him a robber (*John* 18:40). When Pilate gave the people the choice between Christ and Barabbas, they voted unanimously for Barabbas: 'Not this man, but Barabbas!' (*John* 18:40).

The name Barabbas means 'son of a father'. It is possible that he was descended from a family of rabbis. A rabbi or teacher was officially addressed by the name 'father'. He may be described as a 'notable prisoner', an alternative rendering of Matthew 27:16. Whatever his background, we are confronted by a revolutionary who resorted to violence in an attempt to achieve his political ambition – the liberation of his country from Roman rule. He would have become a popular hero the moment he was imprisoned. He stood for the people's ideal. Perhaps Pilate saw Jesus as another kind of revolutionary who claimed to be the 'Christ' or 'Messiah'. Given the choice the people might well agree to release this Jesus who had already suffered so much at the governor's hands. Why not chance it?

It would seem from Matthew's account that the people had some time to consider this choice. There was that interruption as Pilate's wife intervened. However, the crowd was not left to make up its mind by itself. The chief priests and elders moved in and persuaded the people to 'ask for Barabbas and destroy Jesus' (*Matt.* 27:20).

So there are two names on the ballot paper, as it were: Jesus and Barabbas. That was a shameful pairing! The Christ of God was placed on the same platform as a sinner and the people must vote for one or the other. Here was a deepening of the Saviour's humiliation. Jesus and Barabbas! The difference between them is infinitely great. Barabbas fights for a political freedom that would be immediate – emancipation from the shackles of Rome. Christ came to deliver from the slavery of sin. Barabbas was popular, the people's man. Christ often antagonized people. He even refused a king's crown from their hand (*John* 6:15). Barabbas preached revolution; Christ preached regeneration. Barabbas was carnal, Christ was spiritual. Barabbas wanted to subjugate; Christ came to serve. Barabbas relied on the sword; Christ had no work for the sword to do.[1] Barabbas sacrificed others; Christ sacrificed himself. Barabbas pleased the human heart; Christ offended it. These were the two names on the ballot paper that day. The choice was stark and clear: Christ or Barabbas?

It is worth noting how Pilate downgraded Christ. To begin with, he placed Christ in a position superior to Barabbas: 'I find no guilt in him' (*John* 18:38). Then he paired Christ with Barabbas: 'The Christ or the criminal, which do you want?' Finally he placed Christ beneath Barabbas as he released the man of violence and flogged the man of righteousness in preparation for death. That ballot was inherently flawed. In reality it was a curse.

Never had the world witnessed so criminal an election. Never has an election been held to decide so momentous an issue. It was a perverse decision as Barabbas was chosen and Christ was rejected. Granted there was a measure of ignorance. Peter could say later, 'I know that you acted in ignorance, as did also your rulers' (*Acts* 3:17). However, that did not render them excusable, and Peter called on them to repent. Granted they could not see the Nazarene as we see him and know him. He stood

---

[1] When our Lord said, 'I have not come to bring peace, but a sword' (*Matt.* 10:34), he indicated that the peace he did bring was not merely the absence of strife, but a peace that would overcome evil, and that would mean conflict of which the sword is a symbol. When Peter in Gethsemane made use of his sword, Christ immediately said, 'Put your sword back into its place. For all who take the sword will perish by the sword' (*Matt.* 26:52). Christ's kingdom is not advanced by force.

before them without form or majesty, and they saw no beauty that they should desire him (*Isa.* 53:2). Pilate's *Ecce Homo*, 'Behold the man' (*John* 19:5), still rings in our ears. There stood the Saviour, crowned with thorns, arrayed in a purple robe – a caricature of royalty – bruised and bleeding, his appearance 'marred beyond human semblance' (*Isa.* 52:14). As Alec Motyer puts it, 'Those who saw him stepped back in horror not only saying, "Is this the Servant?" but, "Is this human?"'[2] Yet the sight of that sorrowful, humiliated figure touched no chord of compassion in their hardened hearts as they cried out again and again, 'Crucify him.'

The very nomination of these two names was a shameful perversion of justice. Priests and people played the political game with Pilate, and in this game all the players lost. History records that Pilate's government ended abruptly as complaints against him reached Rome. He was deposed and exiled and, according to tradition, committed suicide. Barabbas and his men carried on their campaign of violence. Finally Rome lost patience and in AD 70 a large army razed Jerusalem to the ground, destroyed the Holy Place and slaughtered the people.

It is true that the religious leaders had the greater sin, but that did not relieve the people of their responsibility and guilt. Christ had lived and moved in their midst. He had restored broken lives, healed the sick, raised the dead, forgiven sins, replaced despair with hope and fear with

[2] Alec Motyer, *The Prophecy of Isaiah* (Leicester, Inter-Varsity Press, 1993), p. 425.

peace, He had wronged no one. Yet the slogan-driven crowd voted for the release of Barabbas and the death of their Benefactor. They knew full well that they were choosing between a notorious bandit and One who was perfectly righteous. They could not answer Pilate's question, 'Why, what evil has he done?' (*Matt.* 27:23).

> But it was useless to ask the mob for reasons. Their worst passions had been aroused, and they were baying for blood. The question of what to do with Jesus was not to be settled by reasoned examination of the evidence. It had been decided by mob hysteria.[3]

THE ASTOUNDING HATRED
It is sobering to contemplate the intense, astounding hatred shown by priests and people to Christ. How can we account for such hatred? Speaking prophetically in Psalm 35 Christ said, 'Malicious witnesses rise up, they ask me of things I do not know. They repay me evil for good; my soul is bereft . . . [they] hate me without cause' (*Psa.* 35:11–12, 19; see also Psalm 69:4). There were no moral grounds to justify such irrational and intense hatred of the Saviour. On no grounds of justice, or truth, or righteousness could such hatred be understood. In that sense it was groundless and 'without cause'.

Viewed from another angle, however, there were reasons why Christ was the object of such bitter animosity.

---

[3] Leon Morris, *The Gospel According to Matthew* (Grand Rapids, Wm. B. Eerdmans, 1992), p. 706.

1. *Envy*. Pilate 'knew that it was out of envy that they had delivered him up' (*Matt.* 27:18). They were filled with jealousy. 'Who did this carpenter from Nazareth think he was? Who commissioned him to preach and teach and make disciples? From which college had he graduated? Had he not recently entered the city like a king to the cheers of the crowd?' We read that the chief priests had plans to put Lazarus to death as well as Jesus, 'because on account of him many of the Jews were going away and believing in Jesus' (*John* 12: 10–11).

It was after Christ's triumphal entry into Jerusalem that 'the Pharisees said to one another, "You see that you are gaining nothing. Look, the world has gone after him"' (*John* 12:19). They felt threatened by what they saw as the Nazarene's success, and believed themselves to be in danger of losing their influence and control. Envy easily becomes hatred; and it can quickly sour relationships in home and church.

2. *The exposure of their hypocrisy*. Christ's exposure of the hypocrisy of the religious leaders had been devastating. It was an expression of divine anger. Think of those fearful 'woes' recorded in Matthew 23. They follow each other like rapier thrusts:

'Woe to you, scribes and Pharisees, hypocrites! For you build the tombs of the prophets and decorate the monuments of the righteous, saying, If we had lived in the days of our fathers, we would not have taken part with them in shedding the blood of the prophets. Thus you witness against yourselves that you are sons of those who murdered the prophets. Fill up, then, the measure of your fathers. You serpents, you brood of vipers, how are you to escape being sentenced to hell?' (*Matt.* 23: 29–33). He calls them 'blind guides', 'blind fools', 'whitewashed tombs'. He saw them for what they were, ever seeking the praise and admiration of others; loving the place of honour at feasts, the best seats in the synagogue, and reverential greetings in the marketplaces, 'For they preach, but do not practice . . . They do all their deeds to be seen by others' (*Matt.* 23:3,5).

Such words on the lips of Christ must have cut these professional ecclesiastics to the quick. Because they were so false, they hated him. Why did Cain slay his brother Abel? 'Because his own deeds were evil and his brother's righteous' (*1 John* 3:12).

Christ's whole character was a standing condemnation of evil, and evil men hated him with all their heart. For the same reason the world hates the true church. So John in his epistle continues, 'Do not be surprised, brothers, that the world hates you' (*1 John* 3:13). The Saviour's scathing condemnation of the scribes and Pharisees makes chilling reading. Nowhere in all the Bible is the wrath of God more forcefully expressed. Yet there is nothing vindictive in that oft repeated 'Woe'. Look! Suddenly the Saviour weeps and cries out in grief as he foresees the coming destruction of Jerusalem. 'O Jerusalem, Jerusalem... how often would I . . . and you would not!' (*Matt.* 23:37).

3. *Their inability to trap him verbally*. On a number of occasions the religious leaders had approached Christ with apparently innocent questions, while their real intention was to ensnare him by his own words. There was that day when they began by flattering him. 'Teacher, we know that you are true and teach the way of God truthfully and you do not care about anyone's opinion, for you are not swayed by appearances.' They professed a desire to know if it were lawful for them to pay taxes to Caesar. Matthew states that they had previously 'plotted how to entangle him in his talk' and Mark says that they wished to 'trap him in his talk' (*Matt.* 22:15–17; *Mark* 12:13).

Christ was 'aware of their malice' and he responded, 'Why put me to the test, you hypocrites?' His reply that they 'render to Caesar the things that are Caesar's, and to God the things that are God's', silenced them. Their hypocritical cunning was no match for the wisdom of the Son of God. Clearly, then, there were plain reasons why such false men feared and hated this Jesus.

THE ENDEMIC HOSTILITY

Had not Christ enjoyed a measure of popularity for a time? Had not thousands flocked to hear him preach? Had they not wanted to make him their king? Did they not meet him with hosannas ('Save, we pray') at this Passover season? True. Yet this interest and adulation were largely superficial and transient. As the real nature of Christ's claims and teaching became apparent, disillusionment was soon replaced by hostility. The factors, already noted, that helped to fuel this hatred, do not fully account for its intensity. There was a much deeper cause.

This hatred was no passing or transient emotion. It sprang from the heart of fallen man. We say that a disease is endemic when it is prevalent in a race or country. This sinful opposition to the Christ of God is endemic: it has its root deep in the human heart. In every generation it issues in the cry, 'We do not want this man to reign over us' (*Luke* 19:14). 'Away with him, away with him, crucify him' (*John* 19:15).

There was nothing new in such hostility. The Second Psalm makes that so clear. There the rulers of the earth are seen to 'set themselves' and to 'take counsel together, against the LORD and against his anointed [Christ], saying, "Let us burst their bonds apart and cast away their cords from us".' The opening verses of this psalm are quoted in Acts 4:25-26 with reference to the fierce enmity of the world to the Righteous One. Over the centuries that rage does not evaporate; rather it intensifies until the Lord returns and crushes his enemies 'with a rod of iron' dashing them in pieces 'like a potter's vessel' (*Psa.* 2:9).

We see, then, that sin is essentially rebellion against God, and that the antagonism shown to the Saviour is indigenous to the heart of man. Sinful man is a rebel. That rebelliousness is dominant in this present world order. God's law is flouted, his Son ridiculed and his church despised and persecuted. What happened that day before Pilate was simply the concentration and crystallization of that endemic hatred of the Son of God. It was brought into sharp focus as the cry went up, 'Not this man, but Barabbas' (*John* 18:40).

THE INESCAPABLE RESPONSIBILITY

There can be no neutrality in the presence of Christ. Once the gospel is preached in our hearing, we do not have an 'open mind'. The choice confronting that crowd before Pilate made neutrality impossible. They had to vote. So in terms of hearing the gospel, we may say that the ballot papers are handed out daily and hourly: Christ or Barabbas? Barabbas stands for the world's values, methods and goals. Christ stands for the kingdom of God, for righteousness and truth, for grace, mercy and spiritual renewal. In earthly elections, one may abstain from voting, but not in this one. We cannot evade our responsibility. It has to be Christ or Barabbas.

Had you been one of that crowd before Pilate, how would you have voted? Take a long, hard look into your heart before you answer, for as I look into my own heart, I am sure that I, too, would not have voted for Christ. 'No one can say Jesus is Lord except in the Holy Spirit' (*1 Cor.* 12:3). God places the ballot paper in our hands. Where shall I place that 'X'?

Well, Barabbas goes free and leaves the prison still standing behind him. Christ experiences hell in order to break the prison bars and liberate prisoners from the bondage of sin. There is no other liberator. He was despised and rejected by men so that sinners might be

IS IT NOTHING TO YOU?

accepted by a gracious God. As we read this account, we are transported in thought and experience across the centuries and we stand in that raging crowd. There sits Pilate – shifty, uneasy, and defensive. And there stands the Lord Jesus – bruised, bleeding, silent, and yet so kingly. Pilate speaks: 'What shall I do with Jesus who is called Christ?' How does your heart respond? 'Let him be crucified', or 'My Lord and my God!'?

3

Nailed to the Cross

It was a common custom when a criminal was crucified, to placard his crime. This was a brief statement of his offence in the form of an inscription either carried before him on the way to execution or attached to him. It was then fastened to his cross for all to see.

When Christ was crucified, Pilate 'wrote an inscription and put it on the cross. It read, 'Jesus of Nazareth, the King of the Jews' (*John* 19:19). It is noteworthy that Pilate's superscription implied no disgrace: Christ was not charged with any wrong-doing. Pilate simply took advantage of the custom to stigmatize the Jews. He was angry with them. He saw them as the bane of his existence. They had just given him a hard time – especially their leaders. So this inscription above Christ's cross was his expression of deep disdain toward the Jews. It was a mocking and bitterly ironical inscription, his last tilt at the Jews. He virtually said, 'This is the King of the Jews!

This wretched, battered, bleeding figure is their King. Some king!' These were words of scornful derision!

This was the time of the Passover and visitors from many parts of the empire were coming to Jerusalem for the feast. Pilate's statement was written in Hebrew, Greek and Latin. Hebrew was the national language; Greek was the language most widely understood; and Latin was the language of Rome, the conquering power. Pilate wished to give his inscription the greatest publicity possible. Frederic Godet makes the telling comment, 'Jesus, therefore, at the lowest point of His humiliation, was proclaimed Messiah-King in the languages of the three principal peoples of the world.'[1]

Each language had its own history, its own dominant idea, and at Calvary each proclaimed the words and message of Pilate. He had given vent to his feelings. These Jews meant no more to him than this miserable, self-styled king – so many good-for-nothings. The Jews understood the insult. It cut them to the quick. 'Do not write, "The King of the Jews", but rather, "This man said, I am King of the Jews"' (*John* 19:21). Pilate, who had previously been so weak, now stood firm as he responded to the chief priests, 'What I have written I have written'. Note the twice repeated 'I have written', and the perfect tense indicates an accomplished fact.

Behind the hand of Pilate another Hand is writing. Calvin puts it so well:

[1] Frederic Godet, *Commentary on the Gospel of John* (Grand Rapids: Zondervan Publishing House, no date), vol. 2, p. 384.

The providence of God, which guided the pen of Pilate, had a higher object in view. It did not, indeed, occur to Pilate to celebrate Christ as the Author of salvation, and the Nazarene of God, and the King of a chosen people, but God dictated to him the commendation of the Gospel, though he knew not the meaning of what he wrote. It was the same secret guidance of the Spirit that caused the title to be published in three languages; for it is not probable that this was an ordinary practice, but the Lord showed, by this preparatory arrangement, that the time was now at hand, when the name of his Son should be made known throughout the whole earth . . . Pilate's firmness must be ascribed to the providence of God . . . Let us know, therefore, that he was held by a Divine hand, so that he remained unmoved . . . Pilate, though he was a reprobate man, and, in other respects, an instrument of Satan, was nevertheless, by a secret guidance, appointed to be a herald of the Gospel, that he might publish a short summary of it in three languages.[2]

God was speaking in, through and above Pilate, and God says, 'What I have written I have written: Jesus of Nazareth is King: that is final. Amen.' Now the languages used by Pilate are highly significant.

[2] John Calvin, *Commentary on the Gospel According to John,* vol. 2 (Grand Rapids: Wm. B. Eerdmans, 1949), pp. 227–9.

IN LETTERS OF GREEK

Greek was the language of culture. For centuries it had expressed what was considered the highest and noblest in human wisdom. Poetry, philosophy, ethics – all had flowed through the channel of the Greek language. Greece was a land of beauty, art and refinement. It produced some of the world's greatest thinkers, artists and sculptors. Greece was the marvel of all the earth, a land of wisdom, reflection and song. The whole world still feels indebted to the perceived wisdom and glory of ancient Greece. Yes, Greek was the language of culture and this language was written on Christ's cross.

This is significant, for in the realm of beauty, music and art generally, Christ must be acknowledged as King. Greece, with all its earthly wisdom and culture, had no answer to the problem of sin. Its wisdom was spiritually blind. It could not bring light and salvation to a needy world. As we read in 1 Corinthians 1:21, 'The world did not know God through wisdom.' There are those who think that all the world needs is education. But an educated sinner is no less a sinner, as several world wars, and mounting crime and depravity so vividly illustrate. This world's wisdom is godless: it puts man at the centre of things. A. C. Swinburne, in his 'Hymn of Man' parodies the angels' song in his lines:

> *Glory to Man in the highest:*
> *For man is the master of things.*

Beethoven's Ninth Symphony, the 'Choral', is becoming the favoured anthem of the European Union. It differs from previous symphonies in that it contains choral sections. The poem used in the finale is Friedrich Schiller's 'Ode to Joy', written in 1785, just before the French Revolution and originally called 'Ode to Freedom'. It places its hope for mankind in the brotherhood of man, and its God is the pantheistic God of nature. The ninth symphony is glorious music incorporating pernicious philosophy:

> *Joy, spark of immortal flame, daughter of Elysium,*
> *Goddess drunk with ardent fire, we come to your*
> *   holy place.*
> *Let your magic bring together those whom earthly*
> *   laws divide;*
> *That all may live as brothers beneath your wide and*
> *   gentle wing . . .*
> *Every living creature finds joy in nature;*
> *All good and evil come from her.*[3]

The philosophy of the Ode is man-centred. It represents the wisdom that knows not the true God. Beethoven understood and identified himself with that outlook. The Choral Symphony was to be an expression of his spiritual beliefs and a declaration of his hopes for mankind. The humanistic thinkers of Europe today have the same vain hope.

---

[3] Friedrich Schiller, *An die Freude* (*Ode to Freedom*), translated from the German (*The Oxford Book of German Verse*, 1957), p. 149.

When God is left out of our thinking, life becomes meaningless, pointless, worthless. When men and women are schooled in this world's wisdom, and God and his truth given no place in their training, the loss is incalculable and we all suffer. There is a strange kind of arrogance with such professed wisdom. God is discussed in a condescending manner. Once a lady asked Dr Jowett of Balliol College, Oxford, 'What do you think about God?' Jowett replied, 'That, my dear lady, is a very unimportant question; the only thing that signifies is what God thinks about me.'

Sinful man is determined to have a world-and-life view that has no place for God. He sees himself existing in an impersonal environment. He sees a mindless universe without purpose or direction, and sees himself, to quote Cornelius Van Til, as 'something sprung by chance from chance'.[4] The truth is that we live in a personal environment. 'The earth is the LORD's and the fullness thereof, the world and those who dwell therein . . . ' (*Psa.* 24:1). So Van Til comments:

> Man's environment precedes man. God is man's ultimate environment and this environment is completely interpretative of man who is to know himself.[5]

Van Til adds, that man, rejecting this truth

> virtually attributes to himself that which a true

[4] Cornelius Van Til, *The Defense of the Faith* (Philadelphia: Presbyterian and Reformed Publishing Company, 1967), p. 180.
[5] Ibid., p. 42.

Christian theology attributes to the self-contained God. The battle is therefore between the absolutely self-contained God of Christianity and the would-be wholly self-contained mind of the natural man. Between them there can be no compromise.[6]

This proud, man-centred philosophy, that characterizes the present world order, must be swept aside and replaced by humility and repentance if ever man is to be saved. This world's beliefs and cultures are fundamentally flawed and often depraved. This is painfully obvious in much that passes for music, literature, sculpture and art in general. So often there is a rejection of structure and meaning, and frequently there is indecency, even blasphemy. It is radically different in Christ's kingdom where all reality is dedicated to the glory of God. Christ is King: write it in Greek!

IN LETTERS OF LATIN

Latin was the language of government, of jurisprudence, the language of a people and empire which had stood for just law and firm government. Rome, a city set on seven hills, looked out in all directions and ruled the world. The Romans built the world's roads. They established its trade. They made its laws. They conquered some of its wildest peoples. They planted the Roman standard on every shore. They built one of the greatest empires of all time. They had a genius for government, and today many

[6] Ibid., p. 148.

systems of law regard the Roman system as their parent. The language of that majestic law was Latin.

It was written on the cross in Latin that Jesus is King. King of the Jews, yes, and king of the nations, too. God the Father has given the Son the nations as his heritage, and the ends of the earth as his possession. The nations do not recognize this King; but the Father's word to the Son is clear: 'You will break them with a rod of iron and dash them in pieces like a potter's vessel' (*Psa.* 2:9). In vain do 'the kings of the earth set themselves and the rulers take counsel together, against the LORD and against his anointed [Christ], saying, "Let us burst their bonds apart and cast away their cords from us."'

In that great Second Psalm, God is represented as laughing at such futile arrogance, and the psalm closes with a warning to this world's rulers to 'kiss the Son', in submission to him, before his wrath is kindled. All too often, our leaders on formal occasions, in Parliament or at coronations and similar events, will, by a brief religious ceremony, doff the hat to God; but the 'kiss' thus offered more resembles that of Judas than that of the penitent prostitute who kissed the Saviour's feet (*Luke* 7:38). The Bible read on such occasions is soon set aside and God's law openly rejected.

When have we heard God's name mentioned reverently at a party political conference? What a transformation there would be if politicians turned to God, seeking in their legislation and policies to honour his law! No longer could they legitimize such evils as abortion, homosexuality and gambling. Whether our rulers believe it or not, Christ is overruling all things. 'All authority in heaven and on earth' has been given to him (*Matt.* 28:18). Ultimately our rulers are accountable to him. They will stand before the righteous Judge, Christ enthroned. Then all the subterfuge, machination and intrigue that characterize so much political behaviour, will be unmasked and judged. When the LORD comes, he 'will bring to light the things now hidden in darkness and will disclose the purposes of the heart' (*1 Cor.* 4:5). The 'new heaven' and the 'new earth' that Christ will then establish will be, in sharp contrast to this present earth, 'the home of righteousness' (*2 Pet.* 3:13, NIV). Then all evil, injustice and oppression will be for ever abolished! Christ is King: write it in Latin![7]

IN LETTERS OF HEBREW

A few modern versions of the Bible put Aramaic in the place of Hebrew in John 19:20, although in the Greek New Testament it is 'Hebrew'. Those who make this change do so because at that time the people generally spoke Aramaic, a Semitic language distinct from Hebrew. The Lord Jesus probably spoke it, too. Aramaic had long been spoken in North Syria and in Mesopotamia. It came to be widely used for commercial and diplomatic transactions. In the course of time it ousted Hebrew as the spoken language of Palestine. Hebrew ceased to be a spoken language about the fourth-century BC. It

[7] See Appendix B.

remained, however, a known language and was used by the elite and by ecclesiastics. Today many English-speaking people are fluent in such languages as French, Spanish, or German, but they normally use English. To them many European languages are known languages. It was the same in Palestine in our Lord's day. Hebrew was still used in the Synagogue. When the Saviour read from Isaiah 61, in the temple, he was reading Hebrew (*Luke* 4:17–21). A Jewish boy at thirteen years of age was admitted to the religious community through the Bar-Mitzvah ('son of the commandment') ceremony. At that ceremony every Jewish boy was expected to read certain passages from the Hebrew Bible. Admittedly, in some cases (perhaps many), the knowledge of the language may have been limited. The fact remains, however, that Hebrew was still a known language, the classical language of Israel. It was the language of religion, God-given, God-taught religion.

Consequently this writer, and he is not alone, is more comfortable with a strict translation from the Greek – 'having been written in Hebrew' (*John* 19:20). If Pilate's barb was aimed at the chief priests, and it was they who protested at what he wrote, what language would have been more suitable than that of their religion – Hebrew?

For centuries the Hebrews had stood for revealed religion. In their best days they shone like a bright light amid the darkness of the surrounding nations. Their whole history was one of redemption by the power and grace of God. They possessed a knowledge of the true

God which no other people had. Pilate wrote on the cross in the language of the true religion, 'Jesus is King.'

In the realm of religion Christ must be supreme and central. There is no other King and Head of the church. God the Father has appointed the Son 'head over all things to the church' (*Eph*.1:22; 4:15; *Col*.1:18). The church is not a democracy, as is sometimes maintained. She is subject in all things to the rule of her King. Even when church members exercise their vote in selecting elders or calling a minister, they are to do so in the light of the qualifications for office as set forth in Scripture, all of which is the Word of Christ. Keeping the headship of Christ in mind, the church must always seek to be guided by his Word alone, not by popular demand or personal taste, not moving with the times, but relating to the times, showing the relevance of the gospel to all of life.

The church must uphold sound doctrine, biblical worship and purity of life, as directed by her King. That was the position restored at the time of the Reformation, especially in the Calvinistic wing of that great movement. Sadly, as the church at large lost the vision of her kingly Head, she turned to her own devices. The sense of worship was often lost. An element of entertainment crept in. Worship services became 'user-friendly'. The awareness of the awesome majesty and holiness of God vanished, replaced by the 'bright' and 'lively' service. Increased informality often resulted in an over-familiar attitude to the Almighty. Man was pleased: God was not glorified. The joy of worship is real and not to be missed. There should be no place for the dull and the dreary in times of worship. The psalmist could say, 'I was glad when they said to me, "Let us go to the house of the LORD!"' (*Psa.* 122:1). Glad! In church and state alike, we need to cry, 'Now therefore why do you say nothing about bringing the king back?' (*2 Sam.* 19:10). Christ is King: write it in Hebrew!

Christ is a King with many crowns. He is the King of all true wisdom and culture. Without him our understanding, our learning will lack the key that unlocks the meaning of the universe, of this life and of history in general. Christ rules over the nation and, as the Lord of history, he is gathering his people from every land, irrespective of class or colour. The church is often like a boat in stormy waters as she faces the hostility of the world. She must never forget that Christ is at the helm. He alone is her rightful King, the only Law-Giver in the church. Let us be jealous for the crown rights of our King!

Little did Pilate realize how appropriate was his action when he wrote that superscription in Greek, in Latin and in Hebrew – the language of Athens, of Rome and of Jerusalem. There are some who would say that Christ is king of the church, but not king in politics, or business, or science, or education. They would give him a restricted sovereignty. They would run life on two gears, the sacred and the secular, every so often changing from one to the other. They try to live on split-levels, where Christ is and where he is not. But Christ is either King everywhere, or else nowhere. A religion that is unrelated to life is abhorrent to him. This fact is powerfully illustrated in the first chapter of Isaiah's prophecy. To the people of that day who were trying to live on split-levels, their religion having no impact on their daily life, God said, 'when you spread out your hands, I will hide my eyes from you; even though you make many prayers, I will not listen' (*Isa.* 1:15). Christ will not accept a split-level loyalty. He either reigns in your life or he does not. So who reigns in your life? What is the guiding principle of your life? Is it the pursuit of pleasure, or wealth, or fame, or is it the glory of God? The evidence is in your home: the TV programmes watched, the books and magazines read, and the friendships maintained. What is the chief influence in the lives of our children, the Bible or the Internet, the Word of God or the latest dubious best-seller?

On the walls of the ruins of the old Coventry cathedral, which took a direct hit during the blitz in 1940, eight stone plaques are displayed illustrating the theme, 'Hallowed be Thy Name.' The wording is impressive: *In Industry, In the Arts, In the Home, In Commerce, In Suffering, In Government, In Education, In Recreation.* One might wish to add, *In Church.* There is a silent witness to an important truth: God is to be honoured in every sphere of human activity: in all things Christ is to have the pre-eminence. A well-known statement of Abraham Kuyper comes to mind: 'There is not a square inch within the domain of our human life of which the Christ, who is the Sovereign over all, does not say, "Mine."'

4

'Father, Forgive Them'

One of the most gruesome forms of death is crucifixion, a penalty reserved for the lowest of criminals. As the nails are hammered in, the pain is excruciating. It is certainly not a time to expect a man to pray for his tormentors. He would be more likely to utter oaths and curses. Yet there was one man who did pray for his enemies, either when the nails were being driven home or when the cross was raised, and he was Jesus of Nazareth. Luke was the only Evangelist to record what he said: 'Father, forgive them, for they know not what they do' (*Luke* 23:34). These words of the Crucified are often quoted, but not always understood. All seven 'words' of Christ on the cross come from the depths of his spirit and are a revelation of profound truths. So we need to look closely and carefully at this prayer.

QUESTIONS RAISED BY THIS PRAYER
As the hammers fall and the rough nails are driven home, the Saviour speaks clearly and confidently. For whom is

he praying? The soldiers? The Romans? The Jews? Yes, they are all included. 'Ah', say some, 'he was praying for the elect, how could he ask for forgiveness for those who were not elect?' Those who think and speak like that are trying to fit this prayer into a theological system. They have reached this conclusion by a dogmatic route, rather than by a careful study of Scripture. Yes, we accept the doctrine of election. It is clearly taught in Scripture. However, we must beware of trying to squeeze the Scriptures into a system of doctrine. That is an unsound procedure.

We do not wish to dodge the question of how Christ could pray for the forgiveness of all his enemies. Could he possibly pray out of harmony with God's eternal decree? In his great high priestly prayer, he said to his heavenly Father, 'You have given him [Christ] authority, over all flesh, to give eternal life to all whom you have given him' (*John* 17:2). And did he not also say in this same prayer, 'I am not praying for the world but for those whom you have given me, for they are yours' (*John* 17:9)? So how can we see this prayer for forgiveness as embracing all of Christ's enemies? Before answering that question, we need to consider another one.

How do we understand the words, 'for they know not what they do'? Some will say that Christ's persecutors knew well what they were doing. The members of the Sanhedrin knew what they were doing when they concocted false charges against Christ. The whole trial was a travesty of justice in what was reputed to be the highest court of justice!

Pilate knew what he was doing when he weakly handed over to be crucified the One whom he knew to be innocent. He stood self-condemned: 'I find no guilt in this man' (*Luke* 23:4). Yet he sentenced him to be crucified in order to appease the Jews – pragmatic politics! No amount of hand-washing could relieve him of his guilt.

Those who stood before the cross mocking and jeering, spurred on by their religious leaders, knew that the One they reviled had always been their benefactor and friend. When had he ever harmed them?

So how do we understand those words, 'They know not what they do'? Here the words of the Apostle Peter on the day of Pentecost are relevant: 'This Jesus, delivered up according to the definite plan and foreknowledge of God, you crucified and killed by the hands of lawless men' (*Acts* 2:23). What did they know of God's 'plan and foreknowledge', of his eternal purpose that Christ should die as a substitute for sinners? Nothing! They were certainly ignorant of the significance of Christ's sufferings and death. They could not fathom the implications of his act in laying down his life, or see the extent of its consequences. Besides, they had lost the vision of their prophets who knew that the Messiah would come as the Suffering Servant, a truth so graphically portrayed in Isaiah 53. They were looking instead for a political Messiah who would free them from the Roman yoke and restore their national independence. Peter could say to them, 'I know that you acted in ignorance, as did also your rulers' (*Acts* 3:17; see also 1 Corinthians 2:8; 1 Timothy 1:13).

We may think that Peter's words were surprisingly lenient to people like Caiaphas and his fellow-members of the chief-priestly families, who were so determined to have Jesus put to death. But however that may be, here is a proclamation of divine generosity, offering a free pardon to all who took part in the death of Christ, if only they realize their error, confess their sin, and turn to God in repentance.[1]

In a sense Christ's enemies did *not* know what they were doing, yet they were guilty of a great wrong in their hostility to Christ. So Peter continued, 'Repent therefore, and turn again, that your sins may be blotted out' (*Acts* 3:19). We need to realize that there is a real sense in which our sins nailed Christ to that horrible cross: we dare not stand at Calvary as spectators. We are all involved.

THE MEANING OF THIS PRAYER

So what about the doctrine of election? Is Christ opposing God's sovereign decree when he prays for the forgiveness of his enemies – without qualification? All hinges on our understanding of that word rendered 'forgive'.

Its meaning is broader than we might have first realized. It can mean to release someone, or not to execute a sentence at once, not to impose the penalty immediately; in short, to grant a temporary suspension of the sentence.

[1] F. F. Bruce, *Commentary on the Book of Acts* (London: Marshall, Morgan & Scott, 1956), p. 90.

There is a wonderful magnanimity in the Saviour's earnest longing that his enemies be given time and opportunity to repent before the inevitable judgement is executed on their sins. If God, the Judge of all the earth, had done then what man's sin deserved, a fearful and just judgement would have fallen on mankind; but Christ pleads for a suspension of that dreadful sentence.

His prayer is not a plea that conflicts with God's righteous judgement, but is a request for a delay in the execution of the sentence so that sinners might have time to repent, see the enormity of their sin and the wondrous grace of God in his Son.

By his death on the cross, Christ has earned the right to make this request. He has a perfect case to present before his Father. He knocks on his Father's door and confidently asks that he suspend judgement for so heinous a sin. He is not pleading for acquittal, nor is he asking for forgiveness in the sense of remission of sin. If the church for which he dies is to be saved, men and women must be given the time and opportunity to hear the gospel and understand what they are doing when they reject Christ. The Word must explain Golgotha. The world must be told exactly what happened at Calvary. Men and women must hear 'the word of the cross' if, by God's grace, there is to be true repentance and saving faith.

Christ, then, is not praying for a cancellation of the execution of judgement, but rather for postponement of what is sure to come in any case. He asks for a day of grace; and Christ's request is granted.

This prayer of Christ had special significance for the nation of Israel. We recall the parable of the fruitless fig tree. After three years it should have borne fruit. The owner saw it taking up space and using nourishment that could have benefited his other plants. His instruction was clear: 'Cut it down'. The gardener pleaded that it be given more time during which it would be given every encouragement to bear fruit (*Luke* 13:6-9). In this prayer Christ asked for 'one more year', as it were, for these guilty people. Despite three years of his ministry among them, they were his enemies: the people of Jerusalem had rejected and spurned the Son of God. God gave them another 'day' of opportunity. In fact, this opportunity spanned some forty years in which the Jewish nation witnessed the wondrous signs of Pentecost, the ministry of the Apostles attended by miraculous signs – more than ample time to repent and be saved. A remnant of the Jews did repent and were saved, but the vast majority's unbelief precipitated the day of wrath, and in the Roman-Jewish war of AD 66–70, Israel, represented by that unfruitful fig tree, was cut down and Jerusalem was razed to the ground.

That is a lesson to all mankind. As a direct result of Christ's prayer on the cross we live in a day of grace. But this day will not last for ever. Our world is ripe for judgement. God waits. We do not know how long his patience will last. In terms of repentance, the only time we are sure of is today. 'Today, if you hear his voice, do not harden your hearts' (*Psa.* 95:7–8).

In the book of Revelation we hear the cry of 'the souls of those who had been slain for the word of God and for the witness they had borne': 'O Sovereign Lord, holy and true, how long before you judge and avenge our blood on those who dwell on the earth?' (*Rev.* 6:9–10).

As we think of that cry so often made, we have Christ's reassurance: 'And will not God give justice to his elect, who cry to him day and night? Will he delay long over them? I tell you, he will give justice to them speedily' (*Luke* 18:7–8).

Oh, the patience and longsuffering of God as he views this sinful world in the light of the prayer that Christ offered on the cross!

Christ knew that the Father had 'given all judgement to the Son' (*John* 5:22) and in keeping with that fact, he virtually prayed, 'Father, let them go today, for the whole of judgement is my prerogative'. Christ was doing what God had done in Paradise when sin made its first appearance on earth. The full wrath of God was withheld for a time, solely because the Seed of the woman would one day crush the serpent's head. The cross was clearly in view in the mind of God. Apart from that cross no one would have escaped the immediate wrath of God.

Christ's prayer spans the centuries. His cross stands astride the course of history. The day of grace is a reality. Had Christ prayed that all his enemies, (and that is what we all are by nature), be granted remission of sin, then all would have been forgiven in that sense. But he prayed that we might have time to hear the gospel and to repent.[2]

THE IMPLICATIONS OF THIS PRAYER

If, as some suggest, the relevance of this prayer is limited to the soldiers at the cross, or to the Jewish nation, then it has no special relevance for us. It is merely a moving incident in ancient history and at most an example to believers. However in the light of Scripture as a whole, it does have relevance for us. It has profound implications for the church and for the individual.

Implications for the Church

God's waiting must not be seen as inactivity. He is active in Providence. He is in full control of his creation. God reigns. The risen, glorified Redeemer reigns. He has commissioned his church to go by his authority 'and make disciples of all nations, baptizing them in the name

---

[2] This understanding of the words, 'Father forgive them', is strongly advocated by Klaas Schilder, who argues that the Greek here does allow this interpretation, and I have accepted his argument in general. R. C. Trench, in his *Synonyms of the New Testament*, recognizes that *aphiemi*, the word translated 'forgive' in Luke 23:34, can have the sense just noted and that in the Septuagint, the Greek translation of the Old Testament widely in use at that time, it did have that meaning. He cites Isaiah 61:1; Leviticus 25:31,40; 27:24 and Deuteronomy 15:3. J. N. Geldenhuys in his *Commentary on the Gospel of Luke* takes a similar view and F. F. Bruce, virtually does the same when, in his comment on Peter's recognition of the ignorance of the Jews in crucifying Christ, he refers the reader to Geldenhuys' comments on Luke 23:34.

of the Father and of the Son and of the Holy Spirit, teaching them to observe all that I have commanded you' (*Matt.* 28:19-20). And he has promised to be with his church 'to the end of the age'. Full use must be made of the day of grace. Time is precious. In the Epistle to the Romans we read that 'everyone who calls on the name of the Lord will be saved'. That affirmation is followed by pertinent questions. 'But how are they to call on him in whom they have not believed? And how are they to believe in him of whom they have not heard? And how are they to hear without someone preaching? And how are they to preach unless they are sent?' (*Rom.* 10:13–15). John Murray comments:

> The logical sequence set forth in these . . . verses scarcely needs comment. The main point is that the saving relation to Christ involved in calling on his name is not something that can occur in a vacuum; it occurs only in a context created by proclamation of the gospel on the part of those commissioned to proclaim it. The sequence is therefore: authorized messengers, proclamation, hearing, faith, calling on the Lord's name.[3]

Christ looks on a lost world and he says 'Go'. He has given his church the message that men and women need to hear if they are to be saved. The day of grace is not to be squandered. The most pernicious aspect of the current

---

[3] John Murray, *The Epistle to the Romans,* vol. 2 (Grand Rapids: Wm. B. Eerdmans, 1965), p. 58.

Inter-Faith movement, which speaks of 'other great Faiths', and claims that the Holy Spirit is working in all these ancient religions, is that it runs counter to Christ's command to his church and sounds the death-knell of Christian mission in the historic sense of that term. The idea now put forth that all religions, Christianity included, can learn from each other, is a mark of apostasy and not of faithfulness to the Lord Jesus Christ. It turns a blind eye to the fact that Christianity is radically different from all other religions in that it teaches salvation by grace alone. Man contributes nothing to his redemption: good works are its fruit, not its cause.

Christianity depends for its existence on a risen, living Saviour to be known, trusted, loved and obeyed. Christ insists that he, and he alone, is the way, the truth and the life: there is no other Saviour, no other gospel. Thus we see the uniqueness of Christianity. Religious teachers who lead their people along the broad road of the Inter-Faith Movement are blind leaders of the blind.

Implications for the Individual

Christ's first prayer on the cross has guaranteed a time to repent, to trust in the Saviour and to live to the glory of God. So you must number your days as you consider the cross of Christ. Every new day that God gives you is another opportunity to seek mercy and to know your sins forgiven. God waits, but do not trifle with God.

Stephen, at the time of his martyrdom, prayed for his murderers, 'Lord, do not hold this sin against them' (*Acts*

7:60). On his knees, amid the flying stones, he echoed Christ's prayer on the cross. He prayed for mercy towards his executioners. As F. F. Bruce puts it:

> Before he was finally battered into silence and death, they heard him call aloud, 'Lord, do not put this sin to their account.'[4]

Stephen's prayer was the fruit of Christ's prayer. His killers did have their day of grace, but sadly there is no evidence that many of them used that opportunity to believe in Stephen's Saviour. Not many!

However, the story of Stephen's death introduces us to Saul of Tarsus. Acts 8 begins, 'And Saul approved of his execution'. Indeed those involved in Stephen's martyrdom 'laid down their garments at the feet of a young man named Saul' (*Acts* 7:58). We know how God in mercy dealt with this sworn enemy of his people. Would Paul ever forget that day when he stood and watched approvingly the martyrdom of that lovely Christian, Stephen? Later Paul was to pray, 'Lord, they themselves know that in one synagogue after another I imprisoned and beat those who believed in you. And when the blood of Stephen your witness was being shed, I myself was standing by and approving and watching over the garments of those who killed him' (*Acts* 22:19–20). The Church Father, Augustine, thought that without Stephen's prayer we would not have had Paul. We may not want to go that far, but certainly Stephen's prayer was not in vain.

---

[4] Op. cit., p. 171.

The implications of that first prayer of the Saviour at Calvary cannot be stressed too much. For the time being, God holds back the full expression of his holy judgement of the ungodly. The gospel must be preached to all without distinction to the end of this age. The gospel offer is extended to all. As the *Westminster Shorter Catechism* affirms, 'God's Spirit . . . doth persuade and enable us to embrace Jesus Christ, freely offered to us in the gospel' (Q. 31). Anyone who wants to be saved may be saved, provided that all attempts at self-redemption are abandoned, and that the gospel is believed and obeyed. If you want to be saved you may be saved, but only on the terms of God's gospel.

Christ's prayer on the cross was loud and clear. There is a sense in which, as the centuries pass, its echo seems to grow more faint. Time is running out! The sun will soon go down on the day of grace! God says, 'Behold, now is the favourable time, behold, now is the day of salvation' (*2 Cor.* 6:2). That 'now' is the period of this present day of grace: it is the time of good news and salvation. It places you and the rest of mankind in a position of favour and opportunity, but equally in a position of great accountability.

5

A Soldier Speaks His Mind

He was an officer in the Roman army, serving in a remote corner of the empire. Jerusalem was probably the last place on earth he wanted to be, stationed in a land where the Roman occupation was deeply resented. As an experienced soldier, this man knew that obedience was the outstanding military virtue. That loyalty was certainly put to the test in Jerusalem, especially at the time of the Jewish Passover, when Jews from far and wide crowded the city. Feelings could run high and one never knew what might happen. This year the place was in a ferment. The Jewish religious leaders had arrested a Nazarene who claimed to be a king and spoke as a prophet. They charged him with sedition and arraigned him before Pilate the Roman Governor, demanding that he be put to death! Such an uproar! He had never seen anything like it in Jerusalem before. During this weekend the army would be on a general 'stand-to'. If only he could be back in the peace and quiet of his homeland!

Well, the priests and scribes finally had their way. This Jesus was to be crucified and the centurion knew that two other men, notorious criminals, were to be crucified at the same time. He would never forget those days. The soldiers had their sport, dressing up this self-styled king in a scarlet robe and crown of thorns, with a reed in his hand, and bowing before him in mock obeisance, while spitting at him and striking him with the reed (*Matt.* 27:27–30). Herod and his warriors had already heaped contempt upon the Prisoner (*Luke* 23:11), and those godless priests had ridiculed him. How prophetic are the words of the twenty-second Psalm:

> *But as for me, a worm I am,*
> *and as no man am priz'd:*
> *Reproach of men I am, and by*
> *the people am despis'd.*
> (v. 6, Scottish Metrical Version)

Now the soldiers have completed their task. There is no movement on that centre cross. Those crucified on either side still writhe in agony, still breathe, but this Jesus hangs motionless, lifeless – a corpse on a cross. It was an awkward moment for friend and foe alike, a difficult, bewildering moment. It seemed like a 'dead end'. Where now? What next? No one knew. There is an eerie silence. But listen! Someone is speaking. Step closer and listen. It is the Roman centurion who had supervised the crucifixion. Now he speaks and the Holy Spirit in Scripture has preserved his words. He said two things about the

Crucified. He called him 'a righteous man' (*Luke* 23: 47, KJV) and 'a son of a god' (*Matt.* 27:54, ESV footnote). Most translations render the statement in Matthew 27:54 as 'Truly this was the Son of God', and, in general, commentators agree. It must be remembered, however, that this man was a pagan and it is highly unlikely that his words were a confession of faith like those of Peter when he said 'You are the Christ, the Son of the living God' (*Matt.* 16:16). While the centurion's words recorded in Matthew 27:54 may be rendered 'the Son of God', it seems wiser to take it that he said 'a son of a god': either translation would be in order. The paganism of that day believed in supernatural beings – children of the gods.

A NOTEWORTHY REFLECTION

Consider the scene! A crowd that had been taunting and mocking Christ on his cross, now turns for home smiting their breasts (*Luke* 23:48). They had experienced great terror during those uncanny hours of darkness, from twelve to three o'clock, when normally the sun would have been shining in its brilliance. A great earthquake had rent the rocks and the earth shook beneath their feet (*Matt.* 27:51).

Now, suddenly, they are overcome with a feeling of guilt, even presentiments of approaching calamity. They know that they had hounded the Nazarene, who was clearly innocent, to his death on a cross. They are disturbed, confused, bewildered. They have lost their equilibrium. Their raucous abuse withers on their lips.

Their haughty mockery has been replaced by self-accusation. What next? They do not know. Arrogant hostility has been replaced by panic.

However, there is certainly nothing of repentance in the behaviour of this panic-stricken crowd. They know full well that they have done wrong, but even the acknowledgement of sin is not repentance. How often King Saul said, 'I have sinned', but he never truly repented. So it was with this emotionally disturbed crowd: no sorrow for their sin, no hatred of it, no repentance.

In the midst of all this hysteria and confusion, the spine-chilling darkness and heaving earth, this unnamed centurion was deep in thought. His words were the product of reflection, and not of emotion. Mark tells us that he had taken note of the manner in which Christ had died: he 'saw how he died' (NIV). He saw three men crucified, but one Man fascinated him. He was so utterly different from the others: praying for his enemies, addressing his Father, caring for his mother, blessing a criminal who had previously cursed him – the centurion must have watched and listened in amazement. Klaas Schilder comments, 'The great calm, the mastery, the absence of all that was bitter and ugly, the triumphant trust in God, all had caused him to reflect.'[1]

There were other aspects of this death that were unique. Jesus had apparently died by an act of his will. As he stood opposite the cross (a detail that is clear from Mark's

[1] Klaas Schilder, *Christ Crucified* (Grand Rapids: Wm. B. Eerdmans, 1944), p. 534.

account, 15:39), the centurion heard him say, 'Father, into your hands I commit my spirit!' (*Luke* 23:46). Then he 'bowed his head and gave up (or dismissed) his spirit' (*John* 19:30). This was preceded by a loud cry (*Matt.* 27:50; *Mark* 15:37), probably the word John reports Jesus spoke immediately before his death, 'It is finished' (*John* 19:30). From the standpoint of the centurion these aspects of Jesus' death were most unusual. That loud cry was not a mark of the exhaustion that normally overcame those crucified. The bowing of his head was equally striking, for those crucified usually did the opposite as they gasped for breath. The Saviour's friends and acquaintances looked on from a distance (*Mark* 15:40); they had a general view, but the centurion who was facing Christ noted every detail and reflected on what he saw. Only then did he speak.

AN AMAZING TESTIMONY

He stated his conviction that this Jesus was 'a righteous man'; more than that, 'a son of a god'! It is probable that this soldier had become hardened to the agony and shame of crucifixion. But on this occasion he found himself deeply moved. He had heard the ridicule and abuse directed at this man by priests and people. They had scoffed at his claim that he was 'the Son of God': 'He trusts in God; let him deliver him now, if he desires him. For he said, "I am the Son of God"' (*Matt.* 27:43). The heart of this centurion had not been hardened against the Nazarene, like the hearts of those around him. In his heart he says, 'No, this man was not a scoundrel, not a criminal, not a pretender. This was a righteous man. He was divine, a son of a god'. Matthew tells us that when the centurion finally spoke the other soldiers agreed (*Matt.* 27:54). These hardened soldiers had a conscience that the priests and people apparently lacked.

In those days, the title 'son of a god' was given to the Emperor. The early Christians could have escaped persecution and death simply by saying, 'Caesar is Lord'. But for them 'Jesus is Lord', not Caesar! We must view the centurion's testimony against this background. Here we have an amazing testimony, because in saying what he did, he was in fact glorifying or praising God (*Luke* 23:47). He acknowledged the claims of Christ as genuine. He saw the Nazarene as no mere man; he recognized the presence of the divine, something that the scribes and Pharisees could not and would not do. As Schilder puts it, 'The majesty of the man Christ [Jesus] captivated him so entirely that he gives the same title of honour to this tattered and abused "Jew" which his people reserve for living Caesars, "Son of a god," he calls Him.'[2] He recognized the presence and power of God, an insight granted to him from heaven. Through the horror and shame of that terrible cross, he suddenly saw glory.

This centurion deserves greater credit than he has been given. He does not deride, mock, scorn or blaspheme. Instead, he stands in awe and wonder before that lifeless figure and utters those amazing words. He is not in total

[2] Ibid., p. 535.

darkness. He gives to the Crucified all the glory of which he is capable. On the broad highway of history he has unique significance as, in a sense, he symbolizes the world-vanquishing power of the crucified Son of God. He unreservedly believed in the supernatural and when compared to many present-day theologians, who reject the supernatural as revealed in Scripture, he stands head and shoulders above them.

A MOMENT OF PREPARATION

So the crowd hurry away, fully aware that they are guilty before God. Behind them hangs that lone, despised, crucified figure. What happens now? They were united in blasphemy and hatred, now they tremble with fear – all classes and types. What is happening here? They are no longer in harmony with their leaders. They do not know what to think or do. Even Christ's friends stand afar off trembling. Is the Holy Spirit at work in the hearts of these people? Certainly there are signs of remorse, but nothing to indicate repentance. The seed of the Word has not been planted here. But the ground is being cultivated for the reception of that seed. That seed will be sown on the day of Pentecost when thousands will be converted and genuine repentance will be evident. As a result of the preaching of the Word at Pentecost, three thousand Jews were converted, many of whom, only fifty days before, had cried out, 'Crucify him.' God's Spirit is all-powerful. When in our day crowds tremble before the terrors that can suddenly assail them, that is the time to proclaim the Law of

God, showing the fearful consequences of sin, and to preach the gospel, pointing sinners to the crucified, risen Redeemer.

With Christ nailed to his cross, all boldness on the part of the crowd had ebbed away. The disciples had already fled. Before his arrest, this Christ had been so active. He had preached, pleaded, protested, blessed and condemned, always inciting and provoking reaction. Now he is still. Is this a dead end? No. This is the hour of victory. Christ has hastened to glory. He is placing his credentials before his Father. Pentecost is guaranteed. The salvation of all those given to him before the foundation of the world is assured. It was never in doubt. Christ could not fail. By his death we have life. With his stripes we are healed. There is no such thing as a dead end in the activity of God. That only happens in the experience of those who harden their hearts in unbelief. They have nowhere to run, nowhere to hide, no shelter from the coming storm of the Judgement Day.

Let us step back in time and stand beside the centurion at Calvary. Listen to him. In the mysterious providence of God, he is pointing us to Christ. He did not have the Bible: you have. He did not, so far as we know, hear the gospel preached: you have heard it, perhaps often. He came from a background of paganism: you may have had many spiritual privileges and opportunities.

The task completed, the centurion marches his men back to barracks. If he survived military service, and returned to civilian life at home, he would often have reflected on that unforgettable day at Calvary and that Man on the centre cross. God had granted him a measure of light then that those around him did not have. Did God in the course of time grant him further light? Who knows? God does.

Near the cross of Christ, some believe and some remain in unbelief. Here some are saved and some are lost. If you would have eternal life and go to heaven when you die, then remember that you cannot by-pass the cross. It is here you see your Saviour. It is here your sins are forgiven. It is here you are saved: right here at the cross and nowhere else.

6

Winners and Losers
at Calvary

We seldom think of what Christ was wearing when he went to be crucified. We do know that when the soldiers had finished mocking the One they had dressed in what seemed like royal garments – a caricature of royalty – they 'put his own clothes on him' (*Mark* 15:20). How he was attired as he staggered beneath his cross does not seem important to us. We pay more attention to the clothes in which he was wrapped when as an infant he was laid in a manger (*Luke* 2:7,12). Those swaddling clothes were given to him in the providence of God. Now his clothes, and one garment in particular, are to be taken from him by the special providence of God. He was to be disrobed.

The swaddling clothes may well be regarded as a symbol of his lowliness and poverty as preparation was made to lay him in a manger. Likewise the disrobing of Christ at Golgotha was a significant symbol. Remember what the angel said to the shepherds of Bethlehem when Christ was born: 'This will be a sign for you: you will find the baby wrapped in swaddling cloths and lying in a manger' (*Luke* 2:12). This would be an unmistakable sign; no other newborn babe in Bethlehem would be found in such circumstances. Some thirty-three years later, what sign is given to us? In effect the Bible says to us, 'You shall find your Saviour stripped of all his clothes hanging on a cross.' That this act of disrobing the Son of God was no mere incidental detail, just part of the regular procedure of crucifixion, becomes clear on reflection. Every detail of Christ's suffering is significant and conveys a message to those prepared to stop and think.

THE CLOTHES CHRIST LOST

Ah, the shame of crucifixion as God's well-beloved Son was stripped naked, according to custom, and nailed to a cross, exposed to public view. Think of that! You do not want to look. One's instinct in such an awkward situation is to avert one's gaze. Do not turn away. Face the shocking reality of that hour. 'Behold, the Lamb of God, who takes away the sin of the world' (*John* 1:29). Behold him now, as he was never seen before and as he will never been seen again. Behold the utter shame to which the Lord of glory lovingly submitted as he died for sinners. His nakedness symbolized all the shame that would have been ours for ever in hell and which we so richly deserve because of sin. There is nothing more shameful than sin.

Christ, the substitute for sinners, bore all that shame to the full. Yes, think of that!

It was customary for the soldiers who performed a crucifixion to take the clothing of the executed man. We know that four soldiers crucified the Lord Jesus (*John* 19:23–24). In the plundering of Christ's clothes an ancient prophecy was fulfilled. 'They divide my garments among them, and for my clothing they cast lots' (*Psa.* 22:18). An old Irish commentator and Hebraist, J. G. Murphy, observes: 'This has only a remote bearing on anything known of David's history, but it was literally enacted in the crucifixion of the Messiah.'[1] Having quoted those words from Psalm 22, John adds 'So the soldiers did these things' (*John* 19:24). They acted freely and responsibly, and yet this disrobing of the Saviour was ordained by God. John expressly says that their action was to fulfil the words of Psalm 22:18. The dominating thought here is that God was in full control of all that was happening, not puny man. To the soldiers and those who were observing, this seemed like a very ordinary event. It happened frequently. But behind the soldiers' greedy hands, there was the hand of God.

Now, Christ by his Word wants us to see what his enemies did to him. Behold the Son of God, naked, hanging between two naked criminals, before a jeering, mocking, blaspheming crowd! There was a day when Christ said, 'Foxes have holes, and birds of the air have

[1] J. G. Murphy, *Critical and Exegetical Commentary on the Book of Psalms*. (Minneapolis: James Family Publishing, 1977), p. 176.

nests, but the Son of Man has nowhere to lay his head' (*Matt.* 8:20). He who made all things (*John* 1:3) had neither house nor home. Now, on the cross, he had absolutely nothing, not even his clothes.

It should be remembered that all Christ's suffering was penal. For a sinless person to dwell in this sinful world meant inevitable pain. In addition, Christ was bearing the punishment of our sins. So this nakedness on the cross was part of that punishment.

When in Eden man sinned, his physical nakedness became the symbol of his total shame before a holy God. He felt his shame and looked for covering. Then God in mercy gave him clothes to wear (*Gen.* 3:21).

> Clothing is not the product of the evolution of culture, but it is the thoughtful gift of God's grace. To go naked after God's first act of clothing us, is not to engage in a form of primitive barbarism, but is to become the victim of retrogression; it is to fall from the plane of life in Paradise.[2]

That clothing of our first parents represented God's common grace, his goodness to all. 'The LORD is good to all, and his mercy is over all that he has made' (*Psa.* 145:9). In a day when nudity and semi-nudity are becoming increasingly and shamelessly common, we need to regard it as another symptom of man's rebellion against God. Nakedness in public is a shame and a sin, a wicked retrogression.

[2] Klaas Schilder, *Christ Crucified* (Grand Rapids: Wm. B. Eerdmans, 1944), p. 170.

Now as we see our dear Saviour disrobed, we must realize that 'God could put clothing on the first Adam only because he would one day take it off the second Adam'.[3] Christ was to suffer for Adam's sin and for all whom the Father had given him, and he must bear the full shame and punishment of that sin. So God takes everything from his Son and abandons him. Adam deserved to be abandoned by God; we all do. We have no claims or entitlements as we stand as guilty sinners before the cross. But Christ experienced hell that one day we might be with him in heaven. In order to win all, he had to lose all. If he is to strip 'principalities and powers', the forces of darkness, and triumph over them, he must first be stripped completely and experience the shame of the cross and the unutterable horror of being forsaken by his Father – the inevitable consequence of bearing our sin.

Nothing was accidental in the suffering and death of our Saviour. All was ordained by God. Prophecy, which is meaningless apart from God's foreordination, was fulfilled in every detail. The soldiers divide garments into four lots. They have come to his 'tunic' which was 'seamless, woven in one piece from top to bottom' (*John* 19:23). It was an undergarment usually worn next to the skin.[4] There was no point in rending the seamless robe, so

---

[3] Schilder, op. cit., p. 172.

[4] The distinguished commentator, Frederic Godet, observes that after the removal of this inner garment, 'one is entirely naked'. *Commentary on the Gospel of John* (Grand Rapids: Zondervan Publishing House), vol. 2, p. 385.

they decided to cast lots for it, little realizing how ancient prophecy was being fulfilled to the letter. Our Saviour left little behind him in this world. In earthly terms he was poor when he came into the world, poor when he left it.

So often Christ had made demands. He laid claim to a boat, a beast of burden, a room for the Passover feast. He had entered Jerusalem to cries of 'Hosanna' as the people spread their garments on the road so that their king might pass over them (*Matt.* 21:8-9)! Now his own clothes are removed and divided among the soldiers. What a contrast to a week earlier when he rode into Jerusalem with those 'Hosannas' ringing in his ears! Now the dice is thrown, but there is nothing of chance here: all was foreordained. 'The lot is cast into the lap, but its every decision is from the LORD' (*Prov.* 16:33). Such was the end of a life that at the beginning was honoured by gifts of gold, and frankincense and myrrh. The life of Christ on earth was like that tunic all of a piece, seamless: all was devoted to the glory of God in the salvation of the elect and the overthrow of Satan and his forces.

THE CLOTHES THE SINNER LOSES

Spiritually, the penitent sinner who stands before the cross is stripped naked. The garments in which he had gloried are seen in a new light. Some of these garments call for careful consideration, especially self-righteousness, self-sufficiency and self-will.

Our Lord warned against the spirit of *self-righteousness*. 'Unless your righteousness exceeds that of the scribes and Pharisees, you will never enter the kingdom of heaven' (*Matt.* 5:20). Their righteousness consisted in strict legal correctness, external adherence to the law and external abstinence from what was forbidden. They kept strictly to their code. It was all external and was paraded for the praise of others. It was cold and heartless and lacking in those qualities taught by our Lord in the Beatitudes. Instead of love, kindness and humility there was pride, greed, hardness of heart – in short, self-righteousness. Their hearts were untouched by the love of God. They were graceless men. They were right to keep the law of God, but wrong in the way and spirit in which they kept it, and wrong in adding laws of their own. Like the Pharisee in the temple, their prayers consisted of boasting and self-congratulation. They forgot that 'the LORD sees not as man sees: man looks on the outward appearance, but the LORD looks on the heart' (*1 Sam.* 16:7).

The sin of self-righteousness is natural to the heart of fallen man. He pins his hope of going to heaven on the life he lives. He sees himself as decent, honest, kind, generous, and law-abiding. He is not like those perverts, extortionists, crooks and rogues so often described by the media, or living near him. 'Thank God', he says, 'I'm not like them.' That is the spirit that trusts in human merit and believes in self-redemption. The imagined righteousness of such a man is totally unacceptable to God.

This truth is powerfully illustrated in Christ's parable of the king's wedding feast for his son. The king quickly noted among his guests a man who had refused the garment traditionally provided on such occasions, and who had come to the feast in his own garment. His sentence was swift and solemn: 'Bind him hand and foot and cast him into the outer darkness. In that place there will be weeping and gnashing of teeth' (*Matt.* 22:11–13).

At the cross, the convicted sinner sees man-centred self-righteousness as God sees it and confesses, 'We have all become as one who is unclean, and all our righteous deeds are like a polluted garment' (*Isa.* 64:6). At the cross he is completely stripped of that offensive attire. Now he will keep God's law, not in order to obtain salvation, but out of gratitude to the Saviour who bestows salvation. Now he will live, not to please himself or win the praise of others, but to glorify God in all that he does (*1 Cor.* 10:31).

Another garment that the sinner must lose at the cross is that of *self-sufficiency*. Increasingly man sees himself as autonomous, independent, self-determining, accountable to no one but himself. He or she determines what is right and what is wrong, and how and when these terms apply. So the influential existentialist philosopher, Jean-Paul Sartre, wrote:

> Man must create his own essence: it is in throwing himself into the world, suffering there, struggling there, that he gradually defines himself . . . Man cannot will unless he has first understood that he can count on nothing but himself: that he is alone, left alone on earth in the middle of his infinite respon-

sibilities, with neither help nor succour, with no goal but the one he will set for himself, with no destiny but the one he will forge on this earth.[5]

Not much joy or hope there! It is infinitely bleak and utterly false; but this is how sinful man would seek to banish God from his universe. This denial of God is increasingly disseminated by the advocates of the theory of evolution, an attempted explanation of how things began and developed which has no place for God. This unproven theory is increasingly presented as fact in books and television programmes. Liberal theologians who hold to what they term 'theistic evolution' (that God used evolution as a means to creation), either do not accept the historicity of the opening chapters of Genesis, or, if they do, fail to see the incompatibility of those chapters with the evolutionary theory.

For example, according to the evolutionist man is an intelligent animal, the result of many millions of years of evolutionary development. According to Genesis, man appeared fresh from the hand of God, mature and perfect in body, mind and soul: he had no ancestors. According to evolutionists, man represents the high point in the evolutionary process. He is seen as gradually rising, eventually from the ape, to his present intelligence and skill.

According to Genesis, man has crashed, fallen from his once lofty position to his present sinful condition:

[5] Quoted by Annie Cohen-Solal in *Sartre: A Life* (New York: Pantheon Books, 1987), p. 221.

evolutionists have no convincing explanation for the existence of evil, regardless of how they label it. According to evolutionists, death existed on this planet for millions of years before man appeared, whereas Genesis teaches that death entered only after man had sinned and was part of the punishment of sin.

The man-centred philosophy of this fallen world has left its mark on every aspect of man's life. God is given no place in politics, education, medical ethics, or in much of scientific research. In February 2003, the 'Praesidium' of the European Union, consisting of thirteen commissioners, prepared Article 2 of the draft European Constitution as it relates to what is termed 'the liberty and the rights of man'. It was decided to omit any reference to God, not that the mere reference to the Name of God would have any impact on the humanistic philosophy that dominates Europe today. This decision, however, is indicative of the spirit of the age. In its work, the commission made use of a paper prepared by the Socialist Josep Borrell Fontelles entitled, 'Let's Leave God Out of This'.[6] As puny men strut and swagger in the spirit of rebellion against God, they see themselves as lord of all they survey, whereas in fact they are slaves under the dominion of sin and Satan (*John* 8:34; *Rom* 3:9; 6:16).

Self-will is another widely worn garment that the sinner loses at the cross, and it takes many forms. It has been suggested that it was Voltaire who said that God made man in his own image and that ever since man has been

[6] *Daily Telegraph* report, 8 February 2003.

trying to return the compliment. Whoever made the comment, it does contain an element of truth. Ever since the Fall, man has been flattered by the devil's cunning lie, as he contradicted the Word of God, saying to our first parents, 'You will not surely die. For God knows that when you eat of it (the forbidden fruit) your eyes will be opened, and you will be like God, knowing good and evil' (*Gen.* 3: 4-5).

That lie has had a two-fold effect. As just noted, man thinks and behaves as if he were God. Then there is the tendency on the part of many, who confess to a belief in God, however vague, to visualize a God of whom they approve – a God who measures up to the standards that they consider acceptable. So they believe in a God made in their own image – a pocket-sized God. Their God must never do anything that would not meet with their approval, such as sending judgments on the earth like the Flood or destroying the wicked cities of Sodom and Gomorrah for their gross sexual perversions. Above all, their God must never send anyone to hell: somehow all must reach Paradise in the end.

This self-will, intrinsic in man's rebellion against God, pays scant attention to God's law or to the Scriptures. It holds aloft the banner of 'human rights', which is often understood to include man's right to do as he pleases. In reality, it is practical atheism – paying lip service to God and living as if there were no God. That is the end product of seeing God in terms of man's own choosing. Sadly, many true Christians have, at times, taken this path. How often we have heard fellow-Christians say, 'I could never accept the doctrine of predestination and election', or 'Paul was just reflecting the culture of his time; those rules no longer apply.' Saddest of all is the rejection of eternal punishment by some leading evangelical scholars in recent decades, holding instead to the annihilation of the wicked after death – in spite of clear, unequivocal biblical evidence to the contrary! To replace our Lord's teaching about hell with annihilation is good news to those who love their sin. It encourages the outlook that says, 'Take thine ease, eat, drink, and be merry' (*Luke* 12: 19, KJV). In *The Pilgrim's Progress*, Bunyan described Mr Selfwill in these terms: 'He neither cared for man, nor Argument, nor yet Example; what his mind prompted him to, that he would do, and nothing else could he be got to.' That is it in a nutshell.

There are times when Christ must say to his own people: 'For you say, I am rich, I have prospered, and I need nothing, not realizing that you are wretched, pitiable, poor, blind, and naked. I counsel you to buy from me gold refined by fire, so that you may be rich, and white garments so that you may clothe yourself and the shame of your nakedness may not be seen, and salve to anoint your eyes, so that you may see' (*Rev.* 3:17-18).

Christians need to beware lest they tread on that path of self-will, especially in such areas as worship, family life and submission to the authority of Scripture. They must never toy with any of the rags and tatters taken from them at the cross.

THE CLOTHES THE SAVIOUR BESTOWS

Are we distressed at the spectacle of our Saviour in his hour of utter poverty? Yes and no. It was for us that he endured the cross. In 2 Corinthians 8:9 we read, 'For you know the grace of our Lord Jesus Christ, that though he was rich, yet for your sake he became poor, so that you by his poverty might become rich.' There we see the wonder of saving grace defined by Charles Hodge as 'the unmerited, spontaneous love of our Lord Jesus Christ'.[7] Christ impoverished himself utterly that his people might be enriched forever. From the glory of heaven he descended to Calvary and the grave. 'None was richer than He; none became poorer than He.'[8]

This was paradoxical service: the greatest of all became the least of all, and he who clothes everything, retained nothing, that we might be clothed with the perfect, spotless robe of his righteousness. So Paul writes, '. . . not having a righteousness of my own that comes from the law, but that which comes through faith in Christ, the righteousness from God that depends on faith' (*Phil.* 3:9). Again he writes, 'David also speaks of the blessing of the one to whom God counts righteousness apart from works: Blessed are those whose lawless deeds are forgiven, and whose sins are covered' (*Psa.* 32:1; *Rom.* 4:6). There we see that Christ's righteousness is counted or

[7] Charles Hodge, *The Second Epistle to the Corinthians: An Exposition* (London: Banner of Truth Trust, 1959), p. 200.

[8] Philip E. Hughes, *Paul's Second Epistle to the Corinthians* (London: Marshall, Morgan and Scott, 1961), p. 299.

imputed to us. God sees us clothed in Christ's righteousness and so we are said to be 'accepted (or favoured) in the beloved' (*Eph*.1:6, KJV). Our sins are 'covered'. This is not what the world terms 'a cover-up'. To have sin 'covered' is to have amends made for it, and that happened when Christ bore the full punishment of sin. Christ's righteousness in life and in death hides all our transgressions from God's view.

That righteousness of Christ is the wedding garment for every member of Christ's blood-bought church. It is indispensable for acceptance with God (*Matt.* 22:11–12). This clothing the crucified Redeemer bestows on his people is theirs forever. They are repeatedly depicted in the book of Revelation as 'clothed in white robes . . . made white in the blood of the Lamb' (*Rev.* 7:9, 13–14). Those white robes symbolize the spotless righteousness of their Redeemer Jesus Christ. His righteousness covers them, now and forever, from the moment they put their trust in Christ, and for all eternity. And one day the condition of every believer in Jesus will correspond to the perfect standing they enjoy by faith in Christ. One day, as the bride of Christ, they shall be 'without spot or wrinkle or any such thing, that she might be holy and without blemish' (*Eph.* 5:27).

How wonderful to be clothed in the righteousness of Christ! All other coverings in which men trust are tawdry and unavailing. Better be robed now in Christ's righteousness, owning him as Saviour and Lord, than to be disrobed forever in hell.

So the soldiers at Calvary throw the dice for that seamless robe. One of them took it with him. Did he ever wear it? He may well have done so. It cost him nothing, but it would not have been his if Christ had not been crucified. Reflect on that! There were winners and losers that day. Winners and losers at the cross! Some win Christ and are found in him and that precious robe of righteousness is theirs forever. Others despise that garment that has been offered and on the last day earn the King's frown and judgement – cast into outer darkness! So on that last, great Judgement Day, what will you be wearing as you stand before the King?

7

Looking on the One
We Pierced

Outside the walls of Jerusalem three crosses stand out against the skyline. Bodies are still suspended from them. Now the sound of marching feet is heard; a company of soldiers approaches. They stand before one of the crosses, look carefully at the crucified man and concluding that he is still alive, one of their number breaks both his legs with a large mallet. They do the same with another of the crucified, ensuring that both men will soon die.

Now they stand before the centre cross on which the body of Christ hangs. One of his disciples is standing nearby, watching anxiously. He wonders what they will do to that body. He must have breathed a sigh of relief as the soldiers concluded that the man on that cross was already dead. The mallet was not used. Then, to his amazement, one of the soldiers took his spear and thrust it into the Saviour's side. Immediately there came out blood and water (*John* 19:34). The soldier was probably making sure that this man was dead. We recall the Saviour's words 'I lay down my life that I may take it up again. No one takes it from me, but I lay it down of my own accord. I have authority to lay it down, and I have authority to take it up again' (*John* 10:17-18). Christ's life was never at the disposal of man. Did that watching disciple recall the instruction regarding the Paschal lamb: 'You shall not break any of its bones' (*Exod*.12:46), or Psalm 34:20, 'He keeps all his bones, not one of them is broken'? Later he definitely did see what transpired that day in the light of prophecy.

The issuing of blood and water probably indicated a ruptured heart, an evidence of the intensity of the Saviour's anguish. We must be careful not to read too much symbolism into the blood and water, although the words of 1 John 5:6 should not be overlooked: 'This is he who came by water and blood – Jesus Christ, not by the water only but by the water and the blood.'

There John undoubtedly has in mind the heresy of his contemporary Cerinthus, who denied the Incarnation. It is noteworthy that it is only John who records the piercing of the Saviour's side and what followed. When John in his first epistle speaks of Christ coming through or by means of water and blood, he is most likely saying that his baptism in the Jordan and his death on the cross with the shedding of blood were essential parts of his self-manifestation and the means by which his work was accomplished. The shedding of Christ's blood at Calvary brings forgiveness and cleansing from sin to all believing souls. Certainly the blood and water that flowed from his riven side remind us of that precious truth. Further than that it seems wiser not to go.

John is at pains to emphasize the reliability of his account. 'He who saw it has borne witness – his witness is true, and he knows that he is telling the truth – that you also may believe' (*John* 19:35). It is probable that it was John who witnessed this incident and was profoundly impressed by what he saw. John's whole purpose in writing his Gospel was that his readers would believe: 'these are written that you may believe that Jesus is the Christ, the Son of God, and that by believing you may have life in his name' (*John* 20:31).

One thing is certain; the Holy Spirit guided him to record this incident and nothing is recorded in Scripture without reason: there is no padding. Indeed this incident is charged with significance, because John continues, 'These things took place that the Scripture might be fulfilled: "Not one of his bones will be broken". And again another Scripture says, "they will look on him whom they have pierced"' (*John* 19:36–37).

Thinking of the passages in the Old Testament that were fulfilled at that moment, we note that the Passover sacrifice was instituted with the command, concerning the lamb, 'You shall not break any of its bones' (*Exod.* 12:46; *Num.* 9:12). The other Scripture quoted by John is Zechariah 12:10: 'And I will pour out on the house of

David and the inhabitants of Jerusalem a spirit of grace and pleas for mercy, so that, when they look on me, on him whom they have pierced, they shall mourn for him, as one mourns for an only child, and weeps bitterly over him, as one weeps for a firstborn.'

Let us step back some five hundred years before Christ's day, to the time of the prophet Zechariah. As we noted earlier, his name means '*Jehovah remembers*', and that is the theme of his prophecy. The God of the covenant would ever remember his people. He was a God of unalterable holiness and justice. He required whole-hearted and loving obedience to his law, yet he was a God of grace and mercy to the penitent. He would never forsake his chosen children. So Zechariah preached God's law to make his hearers aware of their wickedness, and God's gospel which alone could change their hearts and bring them back to the Lord. This key passage in Zechariah 12, in the context of John's account of the piercing of the body of Christ, calls for prayerful consideration.

A PENITENT LOOK
Zechariah spoke of a time when the people would look on the One they had pierced and 'mourn for him, as one mourns for an only child'; they will 'weep bitterly over him, as one weeps over a first born'. He foresees a deep, heart-rending sorrow on the part of those who had drifted far from God and dishonoured him in their lives. What brings about such a profound change? We read that this great reversal takes place because God pours out

upon the people 'a spirit of grace and pleas for mercy'. Zechariah speaks here of 'the house of David and the inhabitants of Jerusalem'. This does not mean that the whole Jewish nation would repent, but that the true, spiritual descendants of David's line should penitently look to and welcome the Messiah.

We have here a pointer to Pentecost, a future outpouring of the Spirit. Earlier prophets had signalled such an event. Isaiah conveyed God's message: 'I will pour my Spirit upon your offspring, and my blessing on your descendants' (*Isa.* 44:3). Ezekiel speaks of the day when God will pour out his Spirit upon the house of Israel (*Ezek.* 39:29). Joel speaks in similar vein (*Joel* 2:28–3:1). So Zechariah is not alone in conveying this word from God. A day would come when God would pour out his Spirit, not sparingly, but in full measure. The results of that day would be remarkable, including great sorrow for sin and true repentance. Multitudes would look with broken and contrite hearts on the One they had pierced.

It is striking that the Lord God speaks of himself as being 'pierced' by men, for it is he who speaks through Zechariah. What does this mean? After all, God is Spirit. In Leviticus 24:11,16 a verb meaning 'to pierce' is used and is translated 'blasphemed'; its object is 'the name of the LORD'. To 'pierce' God's Name is to profane it. The same meaning may be assumed in the passage in Zechariah. The people had by their disobedience insulted and blasphemed their God.

As John records the literal piercing of the body of Christ, he sees a fulfilment of what was foreshadowed in Zechariah's prophecy, and so he writes, 'These things took place that the Scripture might be fulfilled' (*John* 19:36). That physical piercing of Christ's body was a symbol of a far greater and more intense piercing that he experienced, and which was used by God's Spirit to pierce the consciences of sinners.

> The piercing which more especially caused the mourning, must also have been of a like profound and spiritual kind; it could be nothing less than the heart grief experienced by the Shepherd of Israel on account of the wrongs and indignities He had received from his people. But the Evangelist John, who had a peculiar eye for the symbolical, and was ever seeing the spiritual imaged in the visible, described in the piercing of our Lord's side by the soldier's spear a sign of that other piercing.[1]

John saw in this fulfilment of prophecy a reason to believe (19:35). Frederic Godet says:

> In order to understand clearly what John felt at the moment which he here describes, let us imagine a believing Jew, thoroughly acquainted with the Old Testament, seeing the soldiers approaching who were to break the legs of the three condemned persons. What is to take place with regard to the body of the

[1] Patrick Fairbairn, *Hermeneutical Manual* (Edinburgh, T. & T. Clark, 1858), p. 448.

Messiah, more sacred than the Paschal lamb? And, lo, by a series of unexpected circumstances he sees this body rescued from any brutal operation! The same spear-thrust which spares it the treatment with which it was threatened realizes to the letter that which the prophet had foretold! Were not such signs fitted to strengthen his faith and that of the church?[2]

At Pentecost, as the message of the cross was preached, many were awakened and convicted by the Spirit of God. They were 'cut to the heart' and when they asked the apostles, 'Brothers, what shall we do?', they were told to repent (*Acts* 2:37–38). They must see that their sin had 'pierced' the Saviour, as he bore the full judgement of God on that sin. They must look and mourn. This was no superficial grief. It was at least as deep and intense as that of a parent heart-broken at the death of an only son. They had 'killed the Author of life' (*Acts* 3:15). They had 'despised and rejected' him (*Isa.* 53:3). Now they look on the One they pierced with a look of penitence and with deep sorrow for their awful sin. It was indeed a remark-able reversal: first they pierced the Lord in enmity and rebellion; now they look in utter woe on the One they had pierced.

Repentance was a dominant note in apostolic preach-ing. This has been equally the case in times of revival and spiritual awakening. People begin to see sin as God sees it – rebellion against God. They become aware of the

[2] *Commentary on the Gospel of John* (Grand Rapids: Zondervan Publishing House), vol.2, p. 396.

consequences of sin: 'The soul who sins shall die' (*Ezek.* 18:4, 20). That note of repentance is no longer struck as it once was, not even in many Reformed pulpits. The 'easy believism' of our time does not pierce the sinner's heart, nor does the emotionalism that often passes for evangelism. That note must be recaptured as a matter of urgency if our preaching is to be really effective. Men and women must be made to see the cross through their tears, with 'a godly grief' that 'produces a repentance that leads to salvation' (*2 Cor.* 7:10).

A BELIEVING LOOK

Those who look to the one they pierced, with sorrow for their sin, do so attentively, trustingly. That is the idea in these passages in Zechariah and John. They look in this manner because God has poured upon them 'the spirit of grace and of supplications' (*Zech.* 12:10, KJV). The old unbelief and rebellion are gone. Now they look to the crucified, risen Redeemer in faith, and hope and gratitude. This look is in itself a new attitude. It is no superficial, transient feeling, no easy change. There has been anguish, bitter pain and shame because of sin, followed by a deep and permanent hatred of sin and a yearning for fellowship with God. This is Spirit-wrought repentance. This is the experience of all Christians. Once we saw no beauty in Christ that we should desire him. Now we see him as 'altogether desirable' and can say, 'This is my beloved and this is my friend' (*Song of Sol.* 5:16). We look to the One we pierced through tears of gratitude.

This look of the penitent soul is essentially one of faith. By God's grace we trust in Christ and believe his Word. This faith is no blind leap in the dark. Faith and knowledge are inseparable. We must know who Christ is, and what he has done and has promised to do. Saving faith does not exist in a vacuum of knowledge. There is no point in debating which comes first – repentance or faith. As John Murray well says:

> There is no priority. The faith that is unto salvation is a penitent faith and the repentance that is unto life is a believing repentance . . . True faith is suffused with penitence.[3]

To be saved, you must have experienced this great reversal in your life. You must have seen the glory of God's grace in Christ. You must have glimpsed (for you can never comprehend) the enormity of your sin that pierced the Son of God. And you must have mourned for your sin with grief too deep for words.

We all stand as guilty sinners before the cross. All pride and self-confidence, in terms of salvation, must be abandoned forever. Many look on Christ with scorn and derision. Others view him patronizingly, attributing many virtues to him, seeing him as the flower of humanity, but denying his deity and spurning his redemptive work. That is the ultimate profanity.

[3] John Murray, *Redemption: Accomplished and Applied* (London: Banner of Truth, 1961), pp. 113, 116.

A DESPAIRING LOOK

In the last book of the Bible, we read of a look far different from that of Zechariah's prophecy or John's record. There we read the solemn words: 'Behold, he is coming with the clouds, and every eye will see him, even those who pierced him, and all tribes of the earth will wail on account of him. Even so, Amen' (*Rev.* 1:7).

Now we step forward in time, how far we do not know. The time has not been revealed, but we prepare for an event that is certain to take place – the return of Christ as Judge. The expression 'coming with the clouds' indicates the majesty and glory of the One who appears. In the Bible, clouds are often associated with divine activity. The Lord repeatedly came down to Moses and Israel in a cloud (for example, Numbers 11:25). In Psalm 104:3 we read that God 'makes the clouds his chariot'. Christ had declared to Caiaphas, the high priest, 'I tell you, from now on you will see the Son of Man seated at the right hand of Power and coming on the clouds of heaven' (*Matt.* 26:64). When the Saviour finally ascended, before the watching disciples 'a cloud took him out of their sight' and they received the message from heavenly messengers, 'This Jesus, who was taken up from you into heaven, will come in the same way as you saw him go into heaven' (*Acts* 1:9,11).

In Revelation 14:14 we read of John's vision of 'a white cloud, and seated on the cloud one like a son of man, with a golden crown on his head, and a sharp sickle in his hand'. This echoes similar language about Christ in Daniel 7:13 and emphasizes the majesty, glory and judgement manifested at Christ's return. A crown of gold signifying his royal supremacy has replaced the crown of thorns worn by the Saviour in the day of his humiliation.

This coming of Christ as Judge will be public: 'Every eye will see him.' There will be no escaping or hiding from his majestic appearance. All, without exception, will see him – 'even those who pierced him'. John uses language reminiscent of Zechariah 12:10. All the ungodly whose sin remains will see their Judge. Elsewhere we are told that 'at the name of Jesus every knee shall bow, in heaven and on earth and under the earth, and every tongue confess that Jesus Christ is Lord, to the glory of God the Father' (*Phil.* 2:10–11).

There will be universal acknowledgement of the lordship of Christ, but not all will acknowledge him savingly. On that day there will be no agnostics, no atheists, no cynics. On that day the ungodly shall look on the One they pierced and 'wail on account of him'. The prolonged, anguished wail of the impenitent – a chilling, blood-curdling lament - echoes only in hell. The jeering and mockery of Calvary, that symbolized the world's derision of God's Son, will be replaced by the anguished cry of those who spurned the grace of God as the wrath of divine judgement overwhelms them. Another great reversal! No book in the Bible describes the judgement of the ungodly so vividly as the Book of Revelation. It is

solemn beyond words to read of a day when 'the kings of
the earth and the great ones and the generals and the rich
and the powerful, and everyone, slave and free, hide
themselves in the caves and among the rocks of the mountains, calling to the mountains and rocks, "Fall on us and
hide us from the face of him who is seated on the throne,
and from the wrath of the Lamb, for the great day of their
wrath has come, and who can stand?"' (*Rev.* 6:15–17).

> The utter hopelessness in that dread day of those who
> have rejected the grace of the gospel is expressed in
> the despairing question: 'Who can stand?' This is the
> damning question mark that robs every ungodly life
> of ultimate meaning.[4]

In such passages of Scripture we are shown the
inescapability of the last great day. Then multitudes will
look to Christ with a despairing look. There is a qualita-
tive difference between the penitent cry of someone
convicted of sin by the Holy Spirit, and the dreadful wail
of a lost soul. The contrast between the deep sorrow
described in Zechariah 12:10 and the hopeless despair
described in Revelation 1:7 is infinitely great. The one is
qualified by salvation, the other by damnation. One is
the welcome cry of birth, the other the pitiful groan of
death.

All will look on Christ at his return, but not all in the
same way. Some will look in praise and joy at the Saviour

---

[4] Philip E Hughes, *The Book of Revelation: a Commentary*
(Grand Rapids: Wm. B. Eerdmans, 1990 and Leicester: IVP), p. 92.

they trusted with their soul. Others will look to him in terror as the wrath of a holy God overtakes them. Which will it be for you? There is no need to leave that question unanswered or in doubt. By trusting in Christ alone for salvation, you can be absolutely sure where you will stand on that great Judgement Day, and with the people of God in all ages you will be able to pray: 'Amen, Come, Lord Jesus!'

8

'Crucified, Dead, and Buried'

'Crucified, dead, and buried'; these words from the Apostles' Creed are familiar to millions of Christians worldwide. They are easily repeated, but not so easily comprehended. Between 'dead' and 'buried' there lies a story from which important lessons may be learned; and a story infinitely wondrous follows.

For the complete record of the burial of Christ's body, we need the accounts of all four Gospels. A lifeless body hangs on the centre cross. An honourable burial is the last thing that Christ's enemies intend. The body cannot remain on the cross: this day of crucifixion was the eve of the Sabbath, known as 'the Preparation'. In modern Greek, the word used here for 'preparation' still refers to our Friday. The coming Sabbath was a special Jewish feast. So this corpse must be removed at once. In any event the Law prohibited leaving such a body on a cross overnight (*Deut*. 21:23). So what will happen to Christ's body? At this point the unexpected takes place. Joseph of Arimathaea, a secret disciple of the Saviour for fear of the Jews, approached Pilate with the request that he might 'take away the body of Jesus' (*John* 19:38). This Joseph was a member of the Sanhedrin, the supreme Jewish Council, and is pictured in the Gospels as an honourable, pious, wealthy and highly respected man. Pilate was surprised to learn that Jesus was already dead and having confirmed that it was so, he gave the necessary permission (*Mark* 15:43–45). It took considerable courage for Joseph to make this request as Mark indicates in his account (*Mark* 15:43). He certainly had nothing to gain by it.

Nicodemus, another secret disciple joined Joseph and together they prepared the body for burial. Nicodemus brought spices, 'a mixture of myrrh and aloes'. They bound the body of Jesus in linen cloths, putting the spices between the strips around the body, as was the custom. This they did lavishly, for the spices brought by Nicodemus weighed about seventy-five pounds (*John* 19:39). They 'laid' the body close by in a new, unused tomb hewn out of rock, the property of Joseph (*Matt.* 27:60). This was not burial in our sense of the term; the body was not lowered into the earth. A heavy round stone closed the entrance to the tomb. A tomb that had never known decay and decomposition was a fit resting-place for a body that would not see corruption.

It is striking to think of these two men, never openly associated with Christ, coming forward at great personal risk to give their departed Master an honourable funeral.

In the hours of crisis it is often the Peters who have sworn loyalty to Jesus with big gestures and fullness of self confidence, that disappoint, and it is the secret and quiet followers of the Master (like Joseph, Nicodemus and the women) that do not hesitate to serve him in love – at whatever cost.[1]

Joseph and Nicodemus were not alone in their task of love. A group of women watched from a distance, taking note of where the body was laid. They planned to return and anoint the body with special spices and ointments (*Luke* 23:56). But it would soon be sundown and the Sabbath would begin (the Jewish day began in the evening, see, for example, Genesis 1:5), so that must wait until the Sabbath, the seventh day of the week, ended, at about 6 p.m., the last Sabbath of the old dispensation. So it was 'very early on the first day of the week, when the sun had risen', that Mary Magdalene and Mary the mother of James and Salome, along with some other women, arrived at the tomb to anoint the body (*Mark* 16:1–2; *Luke* 23:55–56). This was done by pouring the oils over the head. It should be noted that spices and aromatic oils were used to offset in some measure the odour from decomposition quickly ensuing after death in that hot climate. There was a sense of finality in all of this: the Master was dead. In this little church funeral – for that is what it really was – all involved had come to pay their last respects.

[1] J. N. Geldenhuys, *Commentary on the Gospel of Luke* (London: Marshall, Morgan & Scott, 1961), p. 619.

LACK OF UNDERSTANDING

During the last few days before the crucifixion, Christ was in the hands of sinners, and how cruel were those hands! In that dread hour Christ could truly pray, 'Rescue me, O my God from the hand of the wicked, from the grasp of the unjust and cruel man' (*Psa.* 71:4). Now, so far as his body is concerned, all is changed, as lovingly and tenderly, and doubtless with tear-filled eyes, Joseph and Nicodemus handle the corpse with reverence and affection.

Yet there is something sadly missing in their hearts and minds. In what spirit are they burying that body? Is it one of expectation or resignation? Are they seeing Christ's death in the whole context of Messianic redemption, or are they simply seeing it as an isolated, heartbreaking event? How well do they know Jesus Christ? Do they think in terms of divinity as they once did? Dazed and bewildered as they undoubtedly were they could not think of the majesty of God as they looked on that lifeless body: that was too much for man's unaided reason. Granted that Joseph and Nicodemus were not members of the apostolic band, yet it is hard to believe that they knew nothing of Christ's repeated teaching about his bodily resurrection.

This obvious lack of understanding is all the more baffling when we observe that Christ's enemies had not forgotten his prediction that he would rise again from the dead. The chief priests and the Pharisees lost no time in going to Pilate saying, 'Sir, we remember how that impostor said, while he was still alive, "After three days I will rise". Therefore order the tomb to be made secure until the third day, lest his disciples go and steal him away and tell the people, "He has risen from the dead", and the last fraud will be worse than the first' (*Matt.* 27:62–64). So a guard of soldiers was provided and the tomb was sealed. These religious leaders now felt that they had defeated any attempt that the disciples might make to remove the body and spread stories of a resurrection. That, however, was the last thing the disciples had in mind and the spirit in which Christ's body was laid to rest illustrates that graphically: they simply were not thinking in terms of resurrection.

Christ's enemies could go to Pilate and say, 'We remember', but his own devoted followers had forgotten! Their hopes were dashed. Their dreams were shattered. Their faith had failed. Like the two on the way to Emmaus, they 'had hoped that he (Jesus) was the one to redeem Israel' (*Luke* 24:21), but it seemed that their hope was an illusion.

At Christ's burial we may see a confession of love, but not a confession of faith. A love that is not joined to true faith is more sentimental than spiritual, very human but not Spirit-wrought. Even in our day, we must be on our guard against a professed love for the Saviour which is largely emotional, a matter of feeling, but lacking in depth and solidity. Heart and mind must be equally involved in our devotion to our dear Saviour.

IMPLICIT DENIAL

In fact the burial of Christ's body had become a total denial of the resurrection. He has been forsaken spiritually as well as physically, although those who conducted the burial were not guilty of the latter. Their previous conduct as secret followers of Christ was a form of denial. Calvin took a strong stand against those termed 'Nicodemites', converts to the Reformed Faith but who maintained a nominal membership in the Roman Catholic church for fear of persecution. Calvin did not approve of the term 'Nicodemite' because of the stand that Nicodemus finally took. To Calvin there was no halfway position between taking a bold stand for the truth and shameful, even cowardly, compromise. Christians, he maintained, should be ready to face death rather than to deny their Lord.

> And all things considered, certainly it is no small condemnation of us to behold what an ardent zeal the holy martyrs had in the past, especially in comparison with the nonchalance we demonstrate. For as soon as a poor man of that time got so much as a little taste of the true knowledge of God, he did not hesitate to expose himself to the danger involved in confessing his faith. He would have preferred to be burned alive than to go so far as to commit some outward act of idolatry. We who have such ample knowledge, which should set us on fire, are cooler than ice. Let us try to justify ourselves of that! But if we do, it will be to heap up more

grievous malediction (curse), and to provoke the ire of God to fall more harshly upon our heads. Let everyone think well on this, each one for himself.[2]

The courage of Joseph of Arimathaea and Nicodemus at the time of Christ's burial is to be acknowledged and admired. Yet in the past their witness and service had been hampered by fear. At this critical moment God took away that fear. That must have been a powerful lesson to them as it should be for us. Through fear these men had in a real sense denied their Lord. We know that Joseph did not agree with the Sanhedrin's attitude to Jesus Christ, and it would seem that he was not present when that court finally condemned Jesus, for the vote was unanimous (*Luke* 23:51; *Mark* 14:64). It is not easy to account for Joseph's absence at that crucial session. One thing is clear, denial of Christ on the part of believers, whatever form it takes, is spiritual weakness resulting from fear because of a lack of faith. David could say, 'In God I trust, I shall not be afraid. What can man do to me?' (*Psa.* 56:11).

However we look at this solemn burial, whether in its forgetfulness of Christ's promise of resurrection, or the frailty of his followers, denial is writ large across the scene – unintentional, but none the less real. It was not to the glory of God. Calvin comments, 'There is then, a fault which is to be condemned'.[3]

---

[2] *Come out from Among Them: Anti-Nicodemite Writings of John Calvin* (Dallas: Protestant Heritage Press, 2001), p. 91f.

[3] John Calvin, Sermon on Matthew 28:1–10, *The Deity of Christ & Other Sermons* (Grand Rapids: Wm. B. Eerdmans, 1950), p. 188.

TOTAL HUMILIATION

The grave was part of the penalty borne by Christ because of our sin. It was part of his humiliation, the deepest point of his humiliation. The *Westminster Shorter Catechism* defines the Saviour's humiliation: 'Christ's humiliation consisted in his being born, and that in low condition, made under the law, undergoing the miseries of this life, the wrath of God, and the cursed death of the cross; in being buried, and continuing under the power of death for a time' (Q. 27). Yes, 'for a time'. Commenting on the statement of the *Westminster Confession of Faith* that the Lord Jesus 'was crucified, and died; was buried, and remained under the power of death, yet saw no corruption', Robert Shaw says:

> Had he revived as soon as he was taken down from the cross, his enemies might have pretended that he was not really dead, and his friends would not have had sufficient evidence that he was actually dead. Therefore, to prove the reality of his death, upon which the hopes and happiness of his people depend, he was laid in a sepulchre, and continued under the power of death for three days and three nights. He was buried, also to sanctify the grave to his followers, that it might be to them a place of repose, where their bodies may rest till the resurrection.[4]

[4] Robert Shaw, *The Reformed Faith: An Exposition of the Westminster Confession of Faith* (Inverness: Christian Focus Publications 1974), p. 105.

Shaw goes on to speak of 'the dreadful malignity and awful desert of sin, which was the procuring cause of the sufferings and death of our Saviour'. It must be remembered that the Lord Jesus voluntarily submitted to that humiliation that began at his birth and ended in the grave. 'He humbled himself by becoming obedient to the point of death, even death on a cross' (*Phil.* 2:8). From the manger to the cross, he followed a path of humiliation. His submission to his Father's will was total and unreserved.

INDISPUTABLE VICTORY

At no point in his redemptive sufferings did our Lord experience defeat. He was confident of victory from the outset. He was never more victorious than in his death and burial. He conquered death in the very act of dying, and, for his people, the grave is a place where Christ has been, the One to whom they are forever united. As the *Heidelberg Catechism* puts it so well, the Christian's 'only comfort in life and death' is 'that I with body and soul both in life and death, am not my own, but belong unto my faithful Saviour Jesus Christ, who, with His precious blood, hath fully satisfied for all my sins' (Q. 1).

In many ways the burial of Christ was unique. He was not 'gathered unto the fathers' like believers throughout the centuries. It was not possible for him to be 'held' by death, he who is the Lord of Life (*Acts* 2:24). His suffering was ordained in accordance with God's eternal plan of redemption, and so were his resurrection and glory.

David, in the Sixteenth Psalm wrote: 'For you will not abandon my soul to Sheol (the grave) or let your holy one see corruption' (*Psa.* 16:10). At Pentecost Peter was quick to point out that David did see corruption, but that he being a prophet 'spoke about the resurrection of Christ' (*Acts* 2:29–31). The grave of Christ was the prelude to resurrection: it was inevitable that death would lose its hold on his body.

The consternation and terror of the men guarding the tomb of Jesus must have been great as the earth shook beneath their feet and they watched as the seal on the tomb broke and 'an angel of the Lord descended from heaven and came and rolled back the stone and sat on it. His appearance was like lightning and his clothing white as snow. And for fear of him the guards trembled and became like dead men' (*Matt.* 28:2–4). They were petrified with sheer terror, completely overwhelmed by what they saw. They were as helpless as dead men.

Well might they tremble! The word translated 'tremble' in Matthew 28:4 is used of the earthquake in chapter 27:51 – 'the earth shook'. These guards were shaken, paralysed by an unearthly fear in the presence of this angelic visitation. Then came the discovery that the tomb was empty: the body of Jesus was nowhere to be seen. The angel had moved the stone so that the tomb might be seen to be empty. Doubtless the soldiers were dismayed.

What would happen to them now? Who would believe their story? After consultation with the chief priests and elders, the soldiers on guard duty were bribed to tell the people that Christ's disciples came by night, while they were asleep, and stole the body of Jesus. A likely story! Matthew records that 'they took the money and did as they were directed', and their story became well known to the Jews (*Matt.* 28:11–15).

Noting the irony in this action of the Jewish authorities, Leon Morris states:

> They had feared that the body might be stolen and resurrection stories circulate on the basis of an empty tomb. They were now ensuring that precisely those stories were circulated, the only difference being that behind the stories was a risen body instead of a stolen body. The Jesus whom they had caused to be slain and put into the tomb was now a living reality, all their bribes and lies could do nothing to alter the facts.[5]

Some liberal theologians say that they believe in the resurrection of Christ in the sense that Paul did. They have 1 Corinthians 15 in mind, implying that Paul did not believe in a *physical* resurrection. Clearly Paul *does* believe in the bodily resurrection of Christ. He mentions his burial, stating that he was 'raised on the third day in accordance with the Scriptures' (verse 4). The whole tenor of that great chapter accords with a bodily resurrection. Frederic Godet writes, 'the dead body laid in the

---

[5] Leon Morris, *The Gospel According to Matthew* (Grand Rapids, Wm. B. Eerdmans, 1992), p. 741–2.

sepulchre disappeared. What became of it? No explanation other than the fact itself of the resurrection has ever been able to account for this mystery.'[6]

In connection with the subject of Christ's resurrection, apart from the testimony of holy Scripture, there is one phenomenon which the sceptic must honestly face. How do we account for the complete transformation of Christ's followers from a state of hopelessness at the time of Christ's burial, to one of total and irrepressible confidence in the resurrection a short time later, and an unshakeable determination to proclaim this truth as of fundamental importance at any cost? We think of a distraught Mary Magdalene, who found the stone removed from the tomb, saying to Peter, 'They have taken the Lord out of the tomb, and we do not know where they have laid him' (*John* 20:2), and then as she meets One whom she thinks is the gardener, her tears flowing freely, she says, 'Sir, if you have carried him away, tell me where you have laid him, and I will take him away' (*John* 20:15). She was looking for a corpse.

We think, also, of those two disciples on the way to Emmaus. They had heard that some women had found the tomb empty when they arrived to anoint the body and had seen a vision of angels who said that Christ was alive. Some had gone to the tomb and confirmed the women's report – 'but him they did not see' (*Luke* 24:24). Were they convinced by what they had heard? Not really. Then

---

[6] Frederic Godet, *Commentary on First Corinthians* (Grand Rapids: Kregel Publications, 1977) p. 759.

there was Thomas, one of the Twelve, who listened to his colleagues saying, 'We have seen the Lord.' Was he convinced? By no means! 'Unless I see in his hands the mark of the nails, and place my finger into the mark of the nails, and place my hand into his side, I will not believe' (*John* 20:24-25). Thomas' scientific mind demanded irrefutable evidence. Could scepticism be more thorough-going? Just think of those frightened disciples huddled behind closed (locked) doors for fear of the Jews (*John* 20:19), men who before long would passionately and joyfully proclaim, 'He is risen!'

How does the sceptic explain this? That they suffered from hallucinations? Does that idea really explain why these men in subsequent years faced persecution and death to proclaim the truth of the resurrection? These were men who 'hazarded their lives for the name of the Lord Jesus Christ' (*Acts* 15:26, KJV)! It was only when Christ was risen and glorified that his disciples understood the 'things that had been written about him and had been done to him' (*John* 12:16). Previously 'they did not understand the Scripture that he must rise from the dead' (John 20:9).

COMFORT FOR CHRISTIANS

Those chosen in Christ from all eternity (*Eph.* 1:4–5) were intimately associated with him as he suffered in their place. At no point did that vital link weaken. So in Romans 6:4 we read, 'We were buried therefore with him by baptism into death, in order that, just as Christ was raised from the dead by the glory of the Father, we too might walk in newness of life. For if we have been united to him in a death like his, we shall certainly be united with him in a resurrection like his.' Here the emphasis is on the union of Christians with the Lord.

> The purpose of bringing this aspect of union with Christ into focus is apparently twofold. It stresses the completeness of identification with Christ in his death – and it prepares for that which is to follow in the latter part of this verse (v. 4), namely, union with Christ in his resurrection. It is burial that gives meaning to resurrection.[7]

We have been entombed with Christ – co-burial with the Redeemer – and we have been raised to 'walk in newness of life'.

R. A. Finlayson makes the following significant comment:

> *The tomb was broken from within!* Never before in the history of mortal man had that happened! Death had reigned supreme; the tomb was its fortress that no man was yet able to storm. Humanity had awaited the approach of death with fearful heart and the grave cast its sombre shadow everywhere. Mary's heart knew it all as she wended her way to the grave, saying to her companion, 'Who shall roll away the stone?' Humanity had been asking that question

[7] John Murray, *The Epistle to the Romans*, vol. 1, (Grand Rapids: Wm. B. Eerdmans, 1965) p. 215.

through the ages, and no hand was strong enough to roll away the stone! But the Resurrection Morning brought new tidings into the experience of men: the stone was rolled away, the tomb was broken, and it was broken from within! . . . It had received an unwonted visitor who broke its seal and snapped its fetters! That is still wonderful tidings to the darkened hearts and sorrowing spirits of men.[8]

In view of Christ's burial and resurrection, the Christian sees death in an altogether different way from that of the unbeliever. Because of the satisfaction rendered by Christ, death has been robbed of its sting for his people (*1 Cor.* 15:54–56). He has atoned for their sins, borne their punishment and deprived the law of its power to accuse and condemn. The Christian lives and dies in the sure hope of a blessed resurrection of the body. When Lazarus died, the Saviour said, 'Our friend Lazarus has fallen asleep' (*John* 11:11). Death was no longer to be seen as a foe to be dreaded. Christ's resurrection would alter all that for his people. It is common in the New Testament to find death referred to as a 'sleep'. A blessed awakening awaits those who die 'in the Lord'. It is interesting to note that the Christian word for a burial place, 'cemetery', denotes 'a place of sleep'.

Every dead body should be treated with respect, particularly that of a Christian. The *Westminster Shorter*

[8] R. A. Finlayson, *A Just God and a Saviour* (Edinburgh: Knox Press, 2002), p. 113.

Catechism, in answer to the question, 'What benefits do believers receive from Christ at death?', states, 'The souls of believers are at their death made perfect in holiness, and do immediately pass into glory; and their bodies, being still united to Christ, do rest in their graves till the resurrection' (Q. 37). In life the body of the Christian is 'a temple of the Holy Spirit' (*1 Cor.* 6:19), and in death that body is 'still united to Christ'. So in 1 Thessalonians 4:14 we read, 'For since we believe that Jesus died and rose again, even so, through Jesus God will bring with him those who have fallen asleep'. That sacred union of the whole person to Christ is never weakened or broken. Therefore the body of a Christian who has 'fallen asleep' must be accorded the utmost respect at all times.

'Crucified, dead, and buried' – not the end for the Lord Jesus, or for his own. The tomb is empty. Christ lives, and because he lives, we also will live (*John* 14:19). But there is another death mentioned in the Bible; it too, involves the whole person and is unending. To live and die in sin and without Christ is to be banished forever from God's immediate presence. This conscious, eternal, tormented state is what the Bible calls 'hell'. But God in mercy and yearning tenderness pleads with your soul, saying, 'As I live, declares the Lord GOD, I have no pleasure in the death of the wicked, but that the wicked turn from his way and live; turn back, turn back from your evil ways, for why will you die?' (*Ezek.* 33:11). Is such grace nothing to you?

9

The Sign of the Rent Veil

Ancient castles, mansions, towers are often impressive, steeped in history, and at times they can be aesthetically satisfying. But there is nothing inherently spiritual about them. In the Bible we read of a building that was not only impressive architecturally, but was in all its aspects unique. It is probably true to say that there never was and never will be an edifice to compare with Solomon's temple. The plan for this first temple came from heaven; in no way was it the product of the human mind. David could say to his son Solomon, as he handed him the plan for the temple, 'All this . . . the LORD made me understand in writing by His hand upon me, all the details of this pattern' (*1 Chron.* 28:19, NASB). God himself was the Architect of that temple. Consequently every detail in this complex and beautiful structure was rich in spiritual symbolism. That temple was modelled on the tabernacle, but the dimensions were double and its ornamentation was richer.

When Moses was commissioned by God to erect the tabernacle, the people of Israel were to make a personal contribution in terms of materials to be used. But the *plan* was God's: 'And let them make me a sanctuary, that I may dwell in their midst. Exactly as I show you concerning the pattern of the tabernacle, and of all its furniture, so you shall make it' (*Exod*. 25:2, 8-9). In Exodus 40 we read of the erection of the tabernacle, and it is significant that as each stage is completed we have the phrase 'as the LORD had commanded Moses'. Likewise every detail of the temple was in accordance with the will of God. Tabernacle and temple alike represented the presence of God among his people and also the sacrificial and redeeming work of the Messiah. Just as the glory of the LORD filled the tabernacle (*Exod*. 40:34), so also that glory filled the temple built and dedicated to God by Solomon (*2 Chron*. 7:1). That glorious edifice was plundered and burned by the Babylonians when they overthrew Jerusalem in 587 BC, robbing it of its sacred vessels, and taking the people captive. In this way the Lord judged his people on account of their persistent disobedience and unfaithfulness.

They had forgotten that while God might condescend in grace to manifest himself to his people, he remained a transcendent God who could not be 'contained' in any earthly structure. As Solomon put it in his prayer at the dedication of the temple, 'But will God indeed dwell on the earth? Behold, heaven and the highest heaven cannot contain you; how much less this house that I have built!' (*1 Kings* 8:27). That was the right perspective.

The temple built by Solomon on Mount Moriah a thousand years before Christ's time on earth, was rebuilt on the same site by Zerubbabel, Ezra and Nehemiah, after the return of the Jews from exile in Babylon. It was replaced by Herod and was still unfinished in our Lord's day. Impressive as these temples were, they were no match for that first temple. The temple was never meant to be an end in itself; it must not become an idol. When one of the disciples admired those great, white stones of the Herodian masonry, saying to Christ, 'Look, Teacher, what wonderful stones and what wonderful buildings!', the Master replied, 'Do you see these great buildings? There will not be left one stone upon another that will not be thrown down' (*Mark* 13:1–2). That took place literally in AD 70 when Jerusalem was destroyed by the legions of Rome. A Muslim shrine, the Dome of the Rock, now occupies the site. 'The God who made the world and everything in it, being Lord of heaven and earth, does not live in temples made by man' (*Acts* 17:24).

When Christ was crucified, there was a dramatic happening that rendered the temple and its elaborate ritual forever redundant.[1] A heavy veil or curtain separated the Most Holy Place from the Holy Place, where the priests entered daily to offer sacrifices. Only the High Priest could enter the Most Holy Place, and that only once a year on the Day of Atonement. Suddenly, that curtain was 'torn in two from top to bottom' (*Matt.* 27:51). This startling occurrence would be immediately apparent

[1] See Appendix A.

to the priests assembled in the Holy Place. Their consternation and fear must have been great, as they looked into the Most Holy Place, which they must never enter and had never hoped to see. And what of its high priest? What were his thoughts as he heard this astounding news? J. C. Ryle says, 'The conscience of Caiaphas, the high priest, must have been hard indeed, if the tidings of that rent veil did not fill him with dismay.'[2]

WHAT THE VEIL SYMBOLIZED

The veil in the temple signified concealment and distance. We are reminded of words in Exodus 20:21 that speak of 'the thick darkness where God was'. At Mount Sinai, when the Law was given, the people, confronted by flashes of lightning, the sound of the trumpet and the mountain smoking, 'stood far off', while Moses drew near. They had a feeling of reverential awe. When the people of Israel crossed the Jordan into Canaan, the priests led the way carrying the Ark of the Covenant which symbolized God's leadership and his presence with them. The command was given 'There shall be a distance between you and it, about 2,000 cubits in length' (*Josh.* 3:4; a cubit was about 18 inches or 45 centimetres).

Israel had the assurance of divine favour and yet there was an awareness of the awful majesty of God. There is a nice balance in the Old Testament between a realization on the part of the Israelites of the inscrutable majesty and

[2] J. C. Ryle, *Expository Thoughts on the Gospel of Matthew* (1856; reprinted Edinburgh: Banner of Truth, 1986), p. 396.

glory of God, and the awareness that he was their God and that they were his people, united by covenant bonds. That is still the case for the people of God. We must never lose that sense of wonder and awe when we stand before the Lord God in worship, yet rejoicing in his covenant love and mercy. That balance must never be lost.

Klaas Schilder states, 'The furnishings of the temple were a delight to the eye; but they spelled out two terrible words: No admittance!'[3] The veil was typical of the exclusion that characterized the whole temple. Heathendom was excluded. The rank and file of Israel were kept at a distance. Between the courts of Israel and that of the Gentiles there was a triple stone wall like that of a fortress, and above it were inscriptions in Greek and Latin warning Gentiles not to enter on pain of death. One of those tablets was discovered by archaeologists in 1871 and was kept in a Baghdad museum. Where precisely it is now, we do not know.

The ornate veil before the Most Holy Place symbolized concealment, distance, exclusion, separation. But there is more. It also symbolized the flesh of Christ's humanity, which in a sense concealed the most excellent glory of the Godhead. The Lord Jesus is the temple of God in perfection. He is Emmanuel, 'God with us'. Although few knew or understood, God dwelt amongst men in the person of Jesus the Nazarene (*1 Tim*. 3:16; *John* 1:14). In him 'the whole fullness of deity dwells bodily' (*Col*. 2:9). Yet there

---

[3] Klaas Schilder, *Christ Crucified*, (Grand Rapids: Wm. B. Eerdmans, 1944), p. 509.

was concealment. It is significant that the veil of the supreme temple of Christ's body and the veil of that lesser temple were rent simultaneously. The veil in the temple was only of symbolical and liturgical significance: the temple it represented was that of the body of Christ, 'the Lamb who was slain' (*Rev.* 5:12). That temple in Jerusalem foreshadowed the priestly office of Christ, as the Epistle to the Hebrews makes abundantly plain.

In Hebrews 10:19–20 we read how we may now enter the holy places 'by the blood of Jesus, by a new and living way, which he hath consecrated for us, through the veil, that is to say, his flesh' (KJV). F. F. Bruce comments, 'If our author knew about the rent veil, its significance was patent to him. But if he did not know about it, his language here drives home the same lesson as the rending of the veil did.'[4]

The incarnation, when the Word was made flesh, was essential to our redemption. It was in his human nature that Christ suffered in our place and overcame the devil (*Heb.* 2:14).

Now that revered veil hangs in two separate pieces. This was no ordinary tear – 'torn from top to bottom' – bisected, no longer a functional curtain. And this was no flimsy curtain. According to the *Mishnah* (the Jewish oral law), the veil was an handbreadth thick, and woven of seventy-two twisted plaits, each plait consisting of twenty-four threads, six threads of each of the four

[4] F. F. Bruce, *Commentary on the Epistle to the Hebrews* (London: Marshall, Morgan & Scott, 1964), p. 246.

Temple-colours: white, scarlet, blue and gold. It measured six feet by thirty and it took three hundred priests to immerse it.[5] That curtain was renewed annually, so this was no threadbare or frayed fabric that was suddenly torn in two.

How did something so startling and improbable happen? Was it caused by the accompanying earthquake? Perhaps – although Matthew records the rending of the veil before mentioning the earthquake. Possible secondary causes aside, this was clearly a miracle. The hand of God rent the veil at the precise moment of the Saviour's death when he 'yielded up his spirit' (*Matt.* 27:50). That torn veil sent forth a powerful message. This was a crucial hour in the history of redemption – Jesus dead on the cross; the veil before the Most Holy Place torn in two! At that time no one saw the connection.

WHY THE VEIL WAS NO LONGER NEEDED

For centuries that veil was the emblem of separation and division. In the temple there was the court of the priests, the court for Jewish men, the court for women and that for Gentiles, with that massive wall excluding Gentiles from entering further. So what did the future hold for mankind in God's purpose? Would God step out from behind that veil? What would make it possible for that

[5] Quoted from the *Mishnah* by Alfred Edersheim, *Sketches of Jewish Social Life* (Peabody: Hendrikson Publishers, Inc. 2001), p. 180. There does not seem to be any reason for doubting the general accuracy of these details from the *Mishnah*.

veil to be no longer required? Well, we have observed that it was at the precise moment of the Saviour's death that the veil was torn from top to bottom. Now that Christ's redemptive work was 'finished', all barriers had been removed for those who trusted in him. Christ's outlook as he went to the cross was global, as was the commission he later gave to the apostles (*Matt.* 28:18–20). Paul stresses the truth that Christ destroyed 'the dividing wall of hostility' that had separated Jew and Gentile. Now in Christ, in terms of spiritual status, there was neither Jew nor Gentile, male nor female (*Eph.* 2:14; *Gal.* 3:28), and we may say, by implication, 'neither black nor white'. We are 'all one in Christ Jesus'. In heaven every class and colour and race will be represented in large measure (*Rev.* 7:9).

What had been legitimate in the past, lingered on as prejudice. It was hard for a Jew to accept that the temple, with its time-honoured barriers and prohibitions, was now redundant having served its purpose. It would take time for Jewish converts to Christianity to accept the radical nature of Christ's priestly work and to realize that he is our great high priest. His sacrifice for sin needs no repetition. The cross on which his sacrifice took place is our altar (*Heb.* 13:10). When we speak thus of the cross, we think of the Saviour's sacrifice. The cross is the true altar.

In our Protestant churches there should be no place for the apparatus of the redundant temple: 'No sacred buildings, no altars, no sacrificing priest'. When Archbishop

Laud came to Scotland with King Charles I in 1633, he was dismayed to find that its inhabitants had 'no religion at all that I could see – which grieved me much'![6] At the time of the Reformation in Scotland, the axe was laid to the root of the tree. A thorough purifying of the church and its worship took place. How easy it is to let impressive buildings and elaborate ritual blind us to the true nature of the church of Christ. J. C. Ryle, first bishop of Liverpool, reminds us, 'The humblest cottage-meeting, where Christ is preached, and the Scriptures honoured, and a few real believers are assembled, is more pleasing in His sight than the grandest cathedral in which the Gospel is never heard and no work of the Spirit ever goes on.'[7]

WHAT THE RENT VEIL SIGNIFIED

Certainly that rent veil indicated the end of the old Jewish religion in the purpose of God. The Gospel door had been flung wide open: 'whosoever will' may come. '"No admittance" could now be erased from God's murals for ever . . . God does the writing and God does the erasing.'[8] However, the rent veil and the divinely-discarded temple of which it was an essential part, had a positive message for the people of God. The Apostle Paul, under the guidance of the Holy Spirit, could assure Gentile Christians that they were 'no longer strangers and aliens' but 'fellow

[6] F. F. Bruce, *Hebrews*, p. 400.

[7] J. C. Ryle, *Charges and Addresses* (1903; reprinted Edinburgh: Banner of Truth, 1978, as *No Uncertain Sound*), p. 177.

[8] Klaas Schilder, *Christ Crucified*. pp. 508, 513.

citizens with the saints and members of the household of God' (*Eph.* 2:19). Paul, the one-time fanatical Pharisee, had come a long way; now in the gospel of Jesus Christ he could embrace Gentile believers in this fashion. The physical barriers in the temple that separated Jew and Gentile were as nothing compared to the utter contempt and disdain in which the Jews held the Gentiles. Now in Christ these deeper and more vicious divisions are abolished.

While it took the early Jewish converts to Christianity some time to come to terms with so radical a change (religiously and culturally), the apostolic message was clear: Gentile believers were 'fellow-citizens with the saints'. They belonged to the people of God. They enjoyed a citizenship greater than that of any earthly city. Then Paul changed his metaphor. Believers are 'built on the foundation of the apostles and prophets'. They are part of a building of which Christ is 'the cornerstone' (*Eph.* 2:20). Christ is that 'tested stone' and 'precious corner stone', the 'sure foundation' foretold by Isaiah (*Isa.* 28:16) and is of crucial importance in this building of which Paul speaks. Paul now took a step further: the church is seen as 'a holy temple in the Lord', 'a dwelling place for God by the Spirit'.

So the tearing up of the old ceremonial system and the abandonment of the temple in Jerusalem, did not constitute a loss for Jews who trusted in Christ. On the contrary, they had gained infinitely more than had been laid aside, as the Epistle to the Hebrews emphasizes over and over again. Now all Christians of whatever nationality must concentrate on simplicity in worship. All that the Mosaic system symbolized is now in Christ enriched, enhanced and gloriously fulfilled. In him we are 'a chosen race, a royal priesthood, a holy nation, a people for his own possession' (*1 Pet.* 2:9).

As we contemplate our inheritance in Christ, we see the uniqueness of his high priestly office. The Jewish high priest could only enter the Most Holy Place with the blood of sacrifice for his own sins and those of the people (*Heb.* 9:7). Christ, the sinless One, 'entered once for all into the holy places, not by means of the blood of goats and calves but by means of his own blood, thus securing an eternal redemption' (*Heb.* 9:12). The Jewish high priest could not offer himself as an atoning sacrifice for sin; Christ could and did. He 'offered himself without blemish to God' (*Heb.* 9.14).

The Old Testament priesthood had many limitations. Christ is the perfect high priest. The service of the Jewish high priest had no intrinsic efficacy. But as John Murray points out, there is

> need for remembering that the work wrought by Christ was in itself intrinsically adequate to meet all exigencies created by our sin and all the demands of God's holiness and justice. Christ discharged the debt of sin. He bore our sins and purged them. He did not make a token payment which God accepts in place of the whole. Our debts are not cancelled; they are

liquidated, Christ procured redemption and therefore he secured it.[9]

In all its aspects, Christ's priestly work is unique, and its consequences permanent and precious beyond our comprehension. Thank God for that torn veil! Just look at our privilege as believers in Christ. 'Therefore, brothers, since we have confidence to enter the holy places by the blood of Jesus, by the new and living way that he opened for us through the curtain, that is through his flesh, and since we have a great high priest over the house of God, let us draw near with a true heart in full assurance of faith' (*Heb.* 10:19-22).

The Apostle Paul speaks of *an inward veil of unbelief* that hindered the Jews from beholding the 'glory of the Lord'. That veil is said to lie 'over their hearts', the very centre and core of their being (*2 Cor.* 3:15). 'But when one turns to the Lord, the veil is removed' (*2 Cor.* 3:16). Paul speaks here from experience: the veil was removed from his heart when, by grace, he turned to Christ in faith. While that passage in 2 Corinthians has special reference to the Jews, many of whom, like Paul, have had that veil removed, it can apply to us all. It is only as we turn to the Saviour, confessing our sin and seeking forgiveness, that the veil is lifted and we behold the glory of the Lord in the face of Jesus Christ.

As you reflect on that far-off historical event in the temple, the centuries seem to shrink in to this present

[9] John Murray, *Redemption: Accomplished and Applied* (London: Banner of Truth, 1961), p. 57–8.

moment. That torn veil is before you. The Hand that tore it is reaching out to you in love and mercy, and a Voice says 'Come to me by my new and living way'. Never have you had a greater opportunity to possess eternal life, and never a greater responsibility.

10

The Sign of the Opened Graves

The Palestine of the New Testament, Jerusalem in particular, has changed dramatically since the time of our Lord. The general physical features remain, the Mount of Olives, the Lake of Gennesaret, the Land of Galilee. All else has changed with the passage of time. For generations Christians have delighted in visiting the 'Holy Land' and have found it an enriching experience. We need to remember, however, that, as Alfred Edersheim observes:

Where the most solemn transactions have taken place; where, if we only knew it, every footstep might be consecrated, and rocks, and caves, and mountain-tops be devoted to the holiest remembrances – we are almost in absolute ignorance of exact localities. In Jerusalem itself even the features of the soil, the valleys, depressions, and hills have changed, or at least lie buried deep under the accumulated ruins of centuries. It almost seems as if the Lord meant to do with the land what Hezekiah had done with the relic of Moses – the brazen serpent when he stamped it to pieces, lest its sacred memories should convert it into an occasion for idolatry.

Then Edersheim makes the following important statement, 'Events, then, not places, spiritual realities, not their outward surroundings, have been given to mankind by the land of Palestine.'[1] That fact needs to be stressed. In this context, events must be seen as infinitely more important than exact geographical locations associated with the movements of our Lord during his earthly ministry.

We have considered the sign of the rent veil, a stunning event embodying a gospel message of supreme importance. That event was either accompanied or closely followed by one that was even more breathtaking. 'And the earth shook, and the rocks were split. The tombs also were opened. And bodies of the saints who had fallen asleep were raised, and coming out of the tombs after his resurrection they went into the holy city and appeared to many' (*Matt.* 27:51–53). This has been helpfully rendered, 'They came out of their tombs, and after Jesus' resurrection they went into the holy city and appeared to many people' (NIV). The resurrection of Christ preceded their appearance in Jerusalem.

---

[1] Alfred Edersheim, *Sketches of Jewish Social Life* (Peabody: Hendrikson Publishers, Inc. 2001), p. 7.

Rock tombs, usually above ground level, like the one in which the body of our Lord was laid, would easily split open in a severe earthquake. This was no ordinary earthquake as the rest of the account makes clear. Once again the hand of God reached out in power to give us another sign that touches the very heart of redemption. In Psalm 104:32 we read that 'the LORD . . . looks on the earth and it trembles'. The modern rationalist smiles at what he sees as an old-world concept: what man could not explain, he attributed to God. But modern man's understanding of the forces of nature resulting in an earthquake in no way alters or weakens the teaching of Psalm 104, that God is the Lord of nature and in full control of his creation, a truth graphically stated in the closing chapters of the book of Job.

When did this earthquake that split open the tombs outside Jerusalem take place? At the precise moment when Christ died. The Saviour had just 'yielded up his spirit' (*Matt.* 27:50). Coincidence? No, God was speaking and continued to speak in what was to follow. He made it clear that Calvary was not just a spot where a certain Nazarene was crucified and that was that – 'end of story'. Far from it. His death on the cross was unique and had colossal implications for all mankind and, indeed, for the whole universe. Well might the earth shake, the tombs open and many saints arise from the sleep of death, all because of what happened at Golgotha. So what do we learn from this sign of the opened graves? What relevance can it have for us some two thousand years later?

THE DEATH OF DEATH

However we look at it, Christ's death was unique. His life did not just ebb away: he did not die of exhaustion. At the moment when he dismissed his spirit, he was in full voice (*Mark* 15:37; *Matt.* 27:50).

It was common for the crucified to be in a state of utter exhaustion in their final moments – not so the Saviour as he spoke in loud tones. He was laying down his life as a sovereign act, giving his life 'as a ransom for many' (*Matt.* 20:28). That word *'for'* indicates the substitutionary nature of Christ's sacrifice.

That ransom ensured the liberation of sinners from the bondage of Satan and sin. Never was Christ more in control of his thoughts and actions than at that moment when as an act of the will he terminated his earthly life (see also John 10:17–18).

The suffering of Christ, culminating in his death, accomplished redemption for his people. We can say with confidence that his death was *the death of death*. Paradoxical as that may seem, it is true to affirm that, by dying as he did, Christ defeated death, and the evidence for that is his resurrection.

So death, described in Scripture as 'the last enemy to be destroyed' (*1 Cor.* 15:26), was defeated by Christ's death and will finally be abolished. Because death has been conquered, it can no longer triumph. So the Christian can say:

> Death is swallowed up in victory
> O death, where is your victory?
> O death, where is your sting?
> (*1 Cor.* 15:54–55).

Because Christ's death atoned for our transgressions, God's law can no longer accuse us and Satan can no longer brandish a broken law in our faces. Now we can begin to see the significance of graves being split open at the precise moment of Christ's death, and many of the saints being raised from the dead.

THE PLEDGE OF THE RESURRECTION

The Jews took the burial of the dead very seriously, and burying-places, which were always outside cities, were to be treated with the utmost respect. It was considered unlawful to eat or drink or walk casually among the tombs. Great must have been the horror of the Jewish leaders when they discovered, after the earthquake, that many of the tombs were split open, and their consternation and fear must have been intense when they discovered that a considerable number of the tombs were empty. What had happened to those bodies? They must have been dumbfounded. Before long they would have the answer.

For the Christian, this sign of the opened graves, with many saints being raised, carries a glorious message. Because of the certainty of Christ's resurrection, this resurrection takes place. Only certain graves were found to be empty that day, the graves of those noted for their piety. God had made a selection among the dead. One was left in death; one was raised to life. Only those united to Christ were raised. So in 1 Corinthians 15:20 we read that 'Christ has been raised from the dead, the first fruits of those who have fallen asleep'. The offering of the first fruits in Old Testament times, symbolized the offering of the entire harvest (*Lev.* 23:10, 17). If Christ is the first fruits, his people must follow him: he is never without his people (*Col.* 1:18). His bodily resurrection guarantees ours because of our union with him.

Christ's death must not be seen in isolation from his resurrection, and the same is true of his resurrection and ours. As Herman Ridderbos comments, 'His resurrection and that of his people form an unbreakable unity.'[2] It has been rightly affirmed that it is the death of Christ which triggers the resurrection of the saints. Calvin reminds us: 'Enoch and Elijah were translated (*ravis*, raptured) without natural death, and were gathered into life incorruptible. But all depends on the resurrection of our Lord Jesus Christ. We must then cling to Him as the first fruits.'[3]

Others, like Lazarus, had been brought back from the dead, but they had to die again. Such resurrections were anticipatory. The resurrection described in Matthew

[2] Herman Ridderbos, *Paul: An Outline of His Theology* (Grand Rapids: Wm. B. Eerdmans, 1975), p. 538.
[3] John Calvin, *The Deity of Christ* (Grand Rapids: Wm. B. Eerdmans, 1950) p. 179.

27:52 was that of a community, and these saints, with glorified bodies, would never taste death again. As William Hendriksen says:

> Everything seems to point to the fact that these saints did not again die. It must be that after they appeared to many for some small period of time, God took them – now body and soul to himself in heaven, where their souls had been previously.[4]

Their bodies were the same as the glorified bodies we shall receive at the final resurrection of the dead when Christ returns. In them we have the earnest and pledge of our resurrection. Christ's death and resurrection ensure the complete redemption of all his people – body and soul.

This sign of the opened graves, with saints being raised, carries an unmistakable message. It is stated succinctly in the *Westminster Larger Catechism*: 'The bodies of the just, by the Spirit of Christ, and by virtue of his resurrection as their Head, shall be raised in power, spiritual, incorruptible, and made like his glorious body' (Q. 87). The Greek word for grave means a *memorial* or *monument*. These opened and vacated graves, are indeed monumental in their silent witness to Christ's victory over death and the certainty of a glorious resurrection day. We note in passing, that at the general resurrection (*Dan.* 12.2; *John* 5:28–29), Christ's people will be raised in

---

[4] William Hendriksen, *The Gospel of Matthew* (Edinburgh: Banner of Truth, 1974), p. 976.

virtue of their union with him, but the wicked will be raised by divine fiat, at the command of God.

THE SUFFICIENCY OF GOD'S WORD

Those saints, raised at the moment of Christ's death, 'appeared' to many in Jerusalem. Did these resurrected saints belong to that small but faithful number of Jews who were 'waiting for the consolation of Israel' (*Luke* 2:25) – people like Simeon and Anna, Zacharias and Elizabeth? Possibly. We do not know if they spoke to those whom they met. But one thing is clear: here in Jerusalem are messengers from the dead, expressly sent by God, with a powerful witness, whether silent or audible. Did multitudes repent? Was the city filled with seeking souls? How many were gathered together in prayer after Christ's ascension? Remarkably, only about 120 believers (*Acts* 1:15).

Our Lord told a parable about how a rich man, suffering the torment of hell, asked Abraham to send Lazarus to his five brothers to warn them of the consequences of an evil life (*Luke* 16:19–31). The exchange between Abraham and the rich man is significant. 'But Abraham said, "They have Moses and the Prophets; let them hear them". And he said, "No, father Abraham but if someone goes to them from the dead, they will repent". He said to him, "If they do not hear Moses and the Prophets, neither will they be convinced if someone should rise from the dead"'. They had the Word of God to teach them the way of salvation. If that did not lead them to repentance, neither would the raising of the dead. The proof of that is seen in Jerusalem when many bodies of the saints were raised and moved openly among the people. Miracles will not change the human heart, as the Gospels make clear (see, for example, John 6:26; 11:53). Only the Word and Spirit of God can do that.

Did Christ show himself to the Jewish leaders after his resurrection? He did not. Why not? They had Moses and the Prophets. Were their hearts changed by the bewildering and supernatural events that preceded and followed Christ's crucifixion, or by the demonstration of spiritual power at Pentecost? Their treatment of Stephen, the first Christian martyr, makes clear that their hearts were as hard as ever and their hatred of the very Name of Jesus more intense (*Acts* 7:54).

God has given powerful signs to his church and to the world: the rent veil of the temple, the opened graves and resurrected saints, and the greatest sign of all, his Son's bodily resurrection. Only the blindness of an unregenerate heart can fail to see the hand of God and hear his voice in such deeds. Christ knew that even his resurrection would not by itself move men and women to saving faith in himself. Was that not in his mind when he concluded his parable with the words, 'neither will they be convinced if someone should rise from the dead'? (*Luke* 16:31). The rest of the New Testament confirms the truth of those words.

We know from the book of Acts and from the Epistles that the church did grow, and that rapidly. How did it happen? How were men and women saved and congregations established? By preaching, preaching, preaching! God used the preaching of his Word to extend and establish his church. There is no special technique of evangelism, no need to add 'attractions' and gimmicks, or seek for mystical experiences. The Apostles have left us an example to follow, as effective now as in their day – the reading and preaching of the Word. They travelled thousands of miles proclaiming the message of the cross and the empty tomb, Christ crucified and risen, mighty to save.

Paul gave instructions that his own epistles be read aloud in the church assemblies (*1 Thess.* 5:27; *Col.* 4:16). The public reading and preaching of the Word go together (*1 Tim.* 4:13), and the Word of God reverently read carries its own unique authority and power. This is the Word which was 'breathed out by God' and therefore, as Paul writes, 'able to make you wise for salvation through faith in Christ Jesus' (*2 Tim.* 3:15-16).

The crying need of the church today is for men who will preach the Word with passionate conviction and in the power of the Holy Spirit. Then hurting churches will heal, many will be saved, Christian fellowships will be formed, the world will take note (*Psa.* 126:2) and above all, God will be glorified.

What he did through the preaching of men like Calvin, Rutherford, Edwards, Whitefield and Spurgeon – to name but a few – he can do again: 'The LORD's hand is not shortened that it cannot save' (*Isa.* 59:1). The hammer of his Word can break the hardest heart (*Jer.* 23:29).

Signs, however wonderful, are signs at best. By themselves they accomplish nothing. But when you read the Bible, or hear it read and expounded, Christ is speaking to you; this is his Word. And God the Father says, '*Hear him*', '*Listen to him*' (*Mark* 9:7). Hear him *now* as he speaks in grace and love; do not wait until he speaks to you in judgement – for it most certainly will be one or the other.

Epilogue
Is It Nothing to You?

'Is it nothing to you, all you who pass by? Look and see if there is any sorrow like my sorrow, which was brought upon me, which the LORD inflicted on the day of his fierce anger' (*Lam.* 1:12). So wrote the prophet, expressing the anguish of Jerusalem at a time when she was experiencing the anger of God for her sins. 'Do you not care? Can you imagine a more painful and shameful punishment?'

As we think of the sorrows of our Saviour and the judgement he bore on behalf of sinners, can we not associate the cry of the prophet with him? The Old Testament prophets looked for the coming of the Messiah. They anticipated the sufferings of Christ. Christ's own knowledge of the Old Testament, his Bible, was perfect and unique. In a real sense he was its author. All Scripture is the Word of Christ and all of it equally authoritative – there is no need to print his actual sayings in red! Those words in Lamentations must have struck a chord deep in the Saviour's heart. Is he not saying to every generation, 'Is it nothing to you, all you who pass by? Look and see if there is any sorrow like my sorrow'?

That question comes to every man and woman who hears the gospel. Is it nothing to you that Christ came into the world to save sinners? Is it nothing to you that he triumphed over Satan and sin and death? Is it nothing to you that he offers full and free forgiveness of sins and eternal life to all who trust in him? Is it nothing to you that he bore the holy wrath of God against sin so that sinners like you might be saved? Some verses by Joseph Addison Alexander, the distinguished Old Testament scholar of Princeton Theological Seminary, bring home to us the solemnity of life and death and the danger of procrastination:

> *There is a time, we know not when,*
>   *A point we know not where,*
> *That marks the destiny of men,*
>   *In glory or despair.*
>
> *There is a line by us unseen,*
>   *That crosses every path,*
> *The hidden boundary between*
>   *God's patience and his wrath.*
>
> *To pass that limit is to die,*
>   *To die as if by stealth;*
> *It does not quench the beaming eye,*
>   *Nor pale the glow of health.*
>
> *The conscience may be still at ease,*
>   *The spirits light and gay;*

That which is pleasing still may please
And care be thrust away . . .

Oh! where is this mysterious bourne
By which our path is crossed;
Beyond which, God himself hath sworn,
That he who goes is lost?

How far may we go on in sin?
How long will God forbear?
Where does hope end, and where begin
The confines of despair?

An answer from the skies is sent,
'Ye that from God depart,
While it is called To-day, repent
And harden not your heart'.

You who pass by, caught up in the rush and pressures of modern society, living a life on earth which, at its longest, is but very brief, being swept steadily and inexorably to eternity and to the judgement of the Last Day – you who pass by –

STOP! LOOK! SEE!
and LIVE!

Appendix A:
Dispensationalism and the Gospel

Those who believe Ezekiel chapters 40–48 teach that one day the Jerusalem temple will be rebuilt and the Levitical ritual of sacrifice restored, fail to grasp the spiritual symbolism of these chapters. Patrick Fairbairn, in his commentary on Ezekiel, quotes Lightfoot to show that the measurements given in this part of the prophecy would, if taken literally, give a temple larger than the earthly Jerusalem, and a Jerusalem larger than all the land of Canaan! Clearly the vision signifies the enlarging of the spiritual Jerusalem and temple, the church, and the blessings of the Christian era. As Fairbairn comments, the idea that the temple and its ritual will yet be restored is not only contrary to the plain teaching of our Lord concerning the total cessation of Jewish worship, and a putting of 'the new wine of the kingdom . . . into the old bottles again', but also 'the most daring denial of the all-sufficiency of the sacrifice of Christ, and of the efficacy of the blood of his atonement'.[1]

[1] Patrick Fairbairn, *An Exposition of Ezekiel* (Minneapolis: Klock and Klock, 1979 reprint), pp. 437, 441–2.

The author of the Epistle to the Hebrews warns his readers of the consequences of returning to the old Levitical system in order to ease the cost of their Christian profession. He shows these Jewish converts to Christianity the uniqueness of the priesthood and sacrifice of Christ, and shows that to compromise the Christian gospel is to lose it. In his classic book, *Prophecy and the Church*, Oswald T. Allis states:

There is only one memorial feast for believers, since the Cross showed so plainly the inadequacy of the blood of bulls and goats, and that is the Holy Supper of the body and blood of Christ, which the Church has observed for centuries and is to keep 'until he come'. The thought is abhorrent that after He comes, the memory of His atoning work will be kept alive in the hearts of believers by a return to the animal sacrifices of the Mosaic law, the performance of which is so emphatically condemned in passages which speak with unmistakable plainness on this very subject.[2]

In this respect, the Epistle to the Hebrews is as strong a rebuttal of modern dispensationalism as it is of Roman Catholicism.

[2] Oswald T. Allis, *Prophecy and the Church* (Philadelphia: Presbyterian and Reformed Publishing Company, 1945), p. 247–8.

Appendix B:
'Righteousness Exalts a Nation'

When this book was being written, a court case between two judges in America was receiving publicity. An Alabama judge had defied a federal court order to remove from the State judicial building a granite plaque on which were engraved the words of the Ten Commandments. The U.S. Supreme Court rejected a request by the Alabama Supreme Court for a last-minute stay to block the federal judge's order, and in due course the offending plaque was removed. The Alabama judge argued that the State should 'acknowledge God as the moral foundation of our law'. The federal judge maintained that this display of the Ten Commandments in a State building violated the constitutional separation of Church and State.

Yet on every American dollar bill and on every coin are the words, 'In God we trust'! Millions of American schoolchildren recite the Pledge to the Flag at the beginning of each day, including the words, 'One nation under God'. The oath taken at an American President's inauguration concludes with the words, 'So help me, God.' In

England a coronation takes place in a cathedral service and the sovereign is handed a Bible with the words, 'Here is the Royal Law.' Yet in our respective countries and elsewhere, our governments often legislate in direct breach of the Law of God.

The case in the States raises a number of important questions. Scripture does see Church and State as two distinct institutions, yet it makes it clear that the State is a divine institution, the civil magistrate deriving his authority from God, being termed 'God's servant' (*Rom*.13:1–7). The idea of a 'neutral State', in moral terms, is a myth. In its legislature, the State either honours the Law of God, or bows to the will of the people. The French philosopher, Jean-Jacques Rousseau, whose views helped pave the way for the French Revolution, insisted that the laws of the State be determined by the will of the people. That view still prevails in our Western society. According to Rousseau, government derives from the consent of the governed, in sharp contrast to Proverbs 8:15–16: 'By me kings reign, and rulers decree what is just; by me princes rule, and nobles, all who govern justly.'

Christians may not agree on the feasibility or the desirability of a Christian State, but the radical difference between biblical teaching in this respect and that of modern humanism must not be ignored. Why are such activities as theft, slander, murder, regarded as crimes and treated accordingly? The Christian answers that they are a breach of the Law of God summarized in the Ten

Commandments. The secularist states that they are unacceptable because they are anti-social.

As we watch lands that once knew the blessings of great spiritual revivals slip steadily into moral decline, does it not become apparent that Reformed Churches have an urgent and increasing obligation to witness to the State? 'Righteousness exalts a nation, but sin is a reproach to any people' (*Prov*. 14:34).